ANECDOTES

OF

GEORGE FREDERICK HANDEL

AND

JOHN CHRISTOPHER SMITH

Da Capo Press Music Reprint Series

MUSIC EDITOR
BEA FRIEDLAND
Ph.D., City University of New York

ANECDOTES

OF

GEORGE FREDERICK HANDEL

AND

JOHN CHRISTOPHER SMITH

WITH

SELECT PIECES OF MUSIC

COMPOSED BY

J. C. SMITH

NEVER BEFORE PUBLISHED

BY

WILLIAM COXE

WITH A NEW INTRODUCTION BY
PERCY M. YOUNG

DA CAPO PRESS · NEW YORK · 1979

Library of Congress Cataloging in Publication Data

Coxe, William, 1747-1828.
  Anecdotes of George Frederick Handel
and John Christopher Smith.

  (Da Capo Press music reprint series)
  Reprint of the 1799 ed. published by W. Bulmer,
London, with a new introduction by Percy M. Young.
  1. Händel, Georg Friedrich, 1685-1759. 2. Smith,
John Christopher, 1712-1795. 3. Composers—Biography.
I. Title.
ML410.H13C87 1979 780'.92'4   79-15128
ISBN 0-306-79512-4

This Da Capo Press edition of *Anecdotes of George Frederick Handel
and John Christopher Smith* is an unabridged republication of
the edition published in London in 1799 by W. Bulmer and Company,
supplemented with a new introduction by Percy M. Young.

Published by Da Capo Press, Inc.
A Subsidiary of Plenum Publishing Corporation
227 West 17th Street, New York, N.Y. 10011

INTRODUCTION

JOHN Christopher Smith — the younger — was one of those generation-linking figures who serve to remind us that separation between cultural eras, and between their exponents, is often apparent rather than real. Smith was born into the baroque in Ansbach, Bavaria and died within an English classical ambience, amid the chaste elegance of Bath. A protégé of his father's part-time employer and friend, George Frideric Handel, Smith lived into and beyond the age of John Christian Bach. He was acquainted with Dr. Henry Harington and Venanzio Rauzzini, worthies of Bath, who entertained Haydn when he visited that city in 1794; and with Daines Barrington who once phrenologically examined the head of the boy Mozart (as also, on another occasion, that of the English infant prodigy, William Crotch). Harington, Barrington, and Crotch were among the Subscribers to the *Anecdotes*. So too was William Gardiner of Leicester, who was the first to sponsor Beethoven's music in England — and that within the lifetime of Smith.[1] The Subscribers also included some with special Handel associations, particularly Lord Malmesbury, son of James Harris of Salisbury, and John Mainwaring, Handel's first biographer.

[1]Beethoven's string trio in E flat (Op. 3) was performed in Leicester in 1794 through Gardiner's good offices. See William Gardiner, *Music and Friends*, London 1838, I, 113.

Mainwaring was not the first author to assume proprietorship of the work of another—though, to give him credit, his *Life of Handel* (1760) did appear anonymously. It was, as will be shown, the result of collaboration with Smith. Thus it is not surprising that much of the substance of the first part of the following *Anecdotes* is familiar from Mainwaring; but it had all been formulated by Smith before Mainwaring's work appeared. Unknowingly, therefore, posterity is greatly in Smith's debt. Without his aid there would have been no *Life of Handel* in 1760, and the subsequent Handel cult would have had a different point of departure. The fact that the book appeared at that time is remarkable—the publication of an "instant" biography immediately after the death of the subject being a modern practice—but Handel was a remarkable man. No one was more aware of this than Smith. But whatever comes from him through Mainwaring, or through his present editor William Coxe, gives also an impression of Handel's ordinariness despite every effort to apotheosize the hero.

It was Smith's fate posthumously to be reduced to the status of a particular kind of non-person: that of a privileged, though dependent, informative acquaintance of a man of genius. In assembling the dual *Anecdotes* Coxe appreciated the unfairness of this by revealing something of Smith's own contribution to his times. In a limited, but still significant, sense, Smith is to be seen as a general *laudator temporis acti*. He knew many persons distinguished in British life and thought, and he made independent forays into various fields of culture. As a composer, performer, and concert director, he fulfilled the aspirations of his German heritage. But, accepting in addition those aims inherent in the elevated Georgian world-view, he overrode the impediments of immigrancy and the limitations attaching to those who practiced music professionally, to become an English savant. That he was one who entertained serious thoughts is indicated by occasional official references to him as the "Rvd Mr. Smith".[2]

Smith was not a clergyman, but he was flanked by those who were. John Mainwaring, Fellow and sometime Bursar of St. John's College, Cambridge, Lady Margaret's Professor of Divinity, and Rector of Church Stretton, Shropshire, and William Coxe, Fellow of King's College, Cambridge, were—so to speak—his literary sponsors. Coxe was Smith's stepson, and it needs to be stated that the doubts once cast on Coxe's responsibility in respect to the

---

[2]Rate Books, City of Bath, 1787–1795; see James S. Hall, "John Christopher Smith (1712–1795)," *Händel-Jahrbuch 1964–1965*, Leipzig 1965, 66.

present work are without foundation.[3] What Coxe did not do, however, was to fill the gaps in his step-father's biography, nor in his pious undertaking did he attempt any kind of critical assessment. This Introduction, therefore, is to be taken as supplementary to Coxe in both respects.

The son of Johann Christoph Schmidt (1683 – 1763), tradesman of Ansbach, and his second wife Susanna, John Christopher (christened Johann Christoph after his father) was born on 7 January 1712. He had an elder sister, Maria Catharina, and, in due course, a younger sister, Margaretha Judith (b. 1713), and brother, Friedrich Philipp (b.1714).[4]

Four years after John Christopher's birth his father, following a visit to Ansbach by Handel, left his native city to join the composer in London. According to the *Anecdotes* Schmidt and Handel had been fellow students in the university in Halle, where, however, there is no official record concerning Schmidt. After leaving Ansbach it was some time before he felt sufficiently secure to uproot his family and settle them permanently in London. By 1720 Smith was engaged in music publishing, his issue of Handel's *Suites de Pieces (sic)* being the first of a number of his friend's works in which he had a commercial interest. In 1722 the Schmidt family was living in Dean Street, Soho, but a year later the business was conducted from Meard's Court, Schmidt working in association with John Cluer. Apart from this enterprise Schmidt served Handel as principal copyist and director of what was to become a considerable team of copyists, and as financial assistant.

John Christopher was eight years of age when his English education began. Either someone had given him preliminary instruction in the English language in Ansbach, or the school which he attended in Soho was strong in the teaching of English as a second language; for after the passage of only a few years the young Smith was associating with some of the most prominent

---

[3]See William C. Smith, "More Handeliana," *Music and Letters* 34, No. 1, 1953, 11. In W. Coxe, *A Historical Tour Through Monmouthshire,* London 1801, there is the following advertisement:

> By the same Author.
> Biographical Anecdotes of HANDEL AND SMITH, in Quarto, with Portraits, and
> Select Pieces of Music, composed by J.C. SMITH, never before published. Price on
> Fine paper £1.4s and on Common Paper, 12s. Published for the Benefit of Mr.
> Smith's Relations.

[4]See Konrad Sasse, "Neue Daten zu Johann Christoph Schmidt," *Händel-Jahrbuch* 1957, 124.

literary figures in London. To have been a young house-guest of John Arbuthnot and to have spoken familiarly with Swift, Pope, Gay, and Congreve was a privilege allowed to few. The result was that Smith became a student of letters, his enthusiasm for which, it may be felt, to some extent conflicted with his musical interests. These were nurtured in the first place by his father. Handel, although prepared to instruct his friend's son in the rudiments of music, somewhat oddly "could not stoop to the drudgery of teaching composition"; so John Christopher went for more advanced instruction to the amiable and scholarly Pepusch and the highly gifted — if temperamental — Irishman, Thomas Roseingrave. At the time Smith was his pupil, Roseingrave published his *Eight Suits of Lessons for the Harpsicord or Spinnet in most of the Keys; with Variety of Passages and Variations throughout the Work.*[5] To the tyro composer this was an inspiration.

Armed with the credentials bestowed by the eminence of his tutors Smith entered the public arena. An early setting of a poem possibly by Arbuthnot, *The Mourning Muse of Alexis,* composed while Smith was Arbuthnot's guest, is extant; but his first published work appeared in 1732 as *Suites de Pieces Pour le Clavecin/Composées par J.C. Smith: Premiere Volume/London Printed for and sold by the Author/In Meards Court near St. Ann's Church Old Soho. And by Thos Cobb at the Engraving and Printing Office in Bow Church-Yard; where all manner of Business is Curiously Engrav'd and Printed.*

For a young man of twenty and an untested composer anxious to advertise his creative faculties, as well as his performing and pedagogic inclinations, Smith was well supported by Subscribers, among whom were numerous notables. On the social side these included Lady Walpole, to whom the volume was dedicated, the Duchess of Newcastle, the Countesses of Plymouth and Walsingham, the Ladies Anne Cavendish, Anna Colliton, and How[e]. Among untitled but socially conspicuous ladies the most notable was one of Handel's greatest admirers and friend, Elizabeth Leigh, sister of Charles Leigh of Adlington, in Cheshire. She subscribed for two volumes. Among artistocratic males Lord Cowper and William Pitt cut lonely figures, harpsichord playing being considered properly an occupation for women and

---

[5]Dedicated to the third Earl of Essex, William Capel, a Gentleman of the Bedchamber to George II, Kepper of St. James's and Hyde Parks, and holder of other offices; published by Walsh c. 1728.

children.[6] Such names as Rudolf Burtschneider, Caroline Diemar, Christopher Ebeling, John Frederick Lampe, John Richard Pachelbel, Charles Weidemann, as well as Pepusch and Handel, indicate the strength of the London German community at the time. In addition to those already named, a large number of eminent London and provincial musicians were represented on the list, including Handel's future librettist Charles Jennens and Henry Carey from the province of literature. Much canvassing preceded publication of young Smith's work, and it is significant that many who had subscribed to Handel's *Admeto* (Cluer, 1727) were among his supporters.

That was a time of vigorous discussion on the nature of opera and how it should be presented to the English. Henry Carey was one of those who addressed himself to the problem and in 1732 wrote the libretto of *Teraminta*. As he himself had studied music with Roseingrave he thought of another Roseingrave pupil to whom he might entrust the setting of his libretto. No doubt Smith's connection with Handel was not thought to be without value. This "New English Opera after the Italian Manner" by Carey and Smith was sponsored by Thomas Arne and performed in the theatre in Lincoln's Inn Fields, on 20, 23, and 30 November 1732. Arne used *Teraminta* to bring to the notice of the public his talented eighteen-year-old daughter, to whom was given the title role. Other performers were Mrs. Barbier, Mrs. Chambers, Miss Jones, and — the only male singer — Mr. Hussey. It was only a few days after *Teraminta* had ended its brief run when Aaron Hill wrote to Handel proposing that he should turn aside from Italian and use the English language in the opera house. Patently a young man in a hurry, Smith now went into partnership with Samuel Humphreys (who had recently added to the libretto for Handel's revived *Esther*) to produce a second opera — *Ulysses*. This had one performance only, also at Lincoln's Inn Fields, on 16 April 1733.

John Walsh issued a second set of harpsichord lessons by Smith about 1735. Albeit shorter than the first, the second list of Subscribers included

---

[6]In his *Principles and Power of Harmony* (1771) Smith's friend Benjamin Stillingfleet devotes a paragraph to this principle:

> *Young ladies should learn music:* To calm the boisterous passions — to relieve the anxieties and care of life — to inspire cheerfulness — to appease the nerves, when irritated by pain, sickness, or labour of mind or body, to soothe the peevishness of infancy and old age — and to raise the mind to a feeling and love of order. She who shall improve the natural talents, with which women are born, of doing all these things, will not have mispent [*sic*] her time by applying three years to music. .

some new and interesting names. Among them were those of Bernard Granville, a conspicuous friend and patron of Handel; John Stanley, the blind musician later to be Smith's partner in the direction of oratorio performances; Thomas Roseingrave, and William Neale and Francis Pacankam (*sic*), indicating a strong Irish interest.

Neale, a music publisher and concert promoter in Dublin, was the proprietor of the Music Hall in Fishamble Street, when a few years later *Messiah* was performed there for the first time. He had shown an interest in Handel earlier, his name being among the Subscribers to *Admeto*. For Pacankam should be read Pakenham, and immediately there is a difficulty. There was at that time no Francis Pakenham. There were, however, two females of the family named Frances. But now comes a further problem. According to the *Anecdotes* (p. 43), in or about 1736 Smith married a sister of Thomas Pakenham. But the family records do not support this, and even in the *Anecdotes* a distinct strain on credibility is imposed in respect to the dowry that never materialized.[7]

Smith became increasingly active in musical affairs in London. In one way or another he helped his father (with whom he was among the founders of the Society of Musicians) and Handel, especially in regard to oratorio performances. In 1740 he made independent entry into this emerging institution. After his *Rosalinda*[8] had been performed in Hickford's "New Great Room," his setting of *David's Lamentation over Saul and Jonathan* — a

[7]Sir Thomas Pakenham (1651–1706), of Pakenham Hall, Co. Westmeath, had five sons and one daughter — Frances — who married George Nugent, of Castle Richard. She died in 1756. The second son of Sir Thomas's eldest son and heir, Edward, was George Edward Pakenham (1714–1768) and he married Frances Vognell of London. Edward was succeeded by Thomas Pakenham (1713 – 1776), who matriculated at Queen's College, Oxford, in 1729, married Elizabeth Cuffe in 1740, and was created first Baron Longford in 1756. He had a sister, Mary, who was married to John Chambers, of Co. Mayo. There is no mention of any other sister. It would seem that the likeliest Pakenham to have subscribed to Smith's publication would have been George Edward Pakenham's wife. George Edward himself was described as a "Hamburgh merchant." See *Burke's Peerage, Baronetage & Knightage*, London 1859.

[8]Advertisement in *An Ode on the Crushing of the Rebellion Anno MDXXXLVI*, J. Lockman:

> ROSALINDA, (dedicated to her Grace the Dutchess [*sic*] of *Newcastle*) perform'd at Mr. *Hickford's Great Room*, near *Golden Square*, by Mr. *Beard*, Mrs. *Arne*, Mr. *Reinhold*, etc. . . Set to Music by Mr. *J.C. Smith*. To which is prefix'd, An Enquiry into the Rise and Progress of Operas and Oratorios, with some Reflections on Lyric Poetry and Music. Sold by *H. Chapelle* [Grosvenor Street]. Price 1s.

fashionable subject at the time — was presented in the same place.[9] John Lockman was responsible for both libretti, and the performances were under the auspices of the Apollo Society, which had also promoted a performance of Handel's *L'Allegro*, directed by Smith.

After the death of his wife, apparently from tuberculosis, Smith seems to have somewhat turned his back on music in favor of more general cultural and artistic endeavors. He was, we are told, reluctant to "live much with the professors of music" — always excepting Pepusch, Roseingrave and Handel, and he was more and more to be found in the congenial company of a group of country gentlemen who wished to become scholars. Coxe, however, is imprecise as to who was with whom, in what place, at any particular time. It is, therefore, convenient to plot the activities of those who exercised considerable influence on Smith and who, in the end, were agents through whom his recollections of Handel (and sometimes his recollections of his father's recollections) were transmitted to John Mainwaring.

In the industrious Coxe's *Literary Life and Select Works of Benjamin Stillingfleet* (1811) there is a more or less adequately dated account of the movements of those who belonged to the little "academy" — in the Renaissance sense — with which Smith became involved.

The key figure was Benjamin Stillingfleet, who in 1737 was dispatched to Europe together with his twenty-year old pupil William Windham, of Felbrig in Norfolk, in order that the young man might complete his education in a manner suitable to a responsible member of the ruling class. Stillingfleet, grandson of a famous bishop, was a Cambridge scholar who had enjoyed life in the country — where he could devote much time to his own intellectual and literary interests — since his engagement as young Windham's tutor fourteen years before the "grand tour" was undertaken. Italy came first, but in due course master and pupil settled on Switzerland as a headquarters. In

---

[9]At the end of Lockman's *Epistle at the Close of the last Session of Parliament* (1746) appeared this advertisement:

> DAVID'S *Lamentation* over SAUL and JONATHAN: An ORATORIO. Set to Music by Mr. *Boyce*, and perform'd by the Gentlemen of the King's Chapel, etc. Afterwards set by Mr. *J.C. Smith*, & perform'd by Mr. *Beard*, Mrs. *Arne*, etc. The fifth Edition. Price 6*d*.

Boyce's oratorio was performed by the Apollo Society at the Devil Tavern, in Fleet Street, on 16 April 1736. For other works on the same subject see "Kritischer Bericht" for Handel's *Saul* (Hallische Händel-Ausgabe, I/13, Leipzig/Kassel 1964), Percy M. Young.

Geneva they spent much time with other members of the group named by Coxe, earnestly discussing literature, art, and music, and a little less earnestly practicing these crafts. A central interest was private theatricals, with or without music. According to the precepts of tourism as then understood, they also joined together in geological, ornithological, and botanical research.

Robert Price, whose father's estate was near Yazor, outside Hereford, claimed descent from the ancient nobility of Wales. He too was sent to Italy, where he conducted his studies quite methodically, practicing landscape drawing under Giovanni Battista Busiri, and musical composition under Andrea Basili, *maestro di capella* of Loreto. Price was an excellent violinist, and composed songs that were described as "remarkably delicate and expressive ... as well as his solos and trios [for instruments] ... in the Italian style."[10] Stillingfleet's opinion was backed by the more expert one of J. C. Smith, whom he had often heard "to observe that Mr. Price was an excellent composer."[11]

In youth Price and Windham complemented each other. The former was a good enough tennis player to have been considered as among the best in Britain; the latter, although "tall, thin and narrow-chested," able to "vie with Price in every feat of strength and agility [and] known through London as boxing Windham."[12]

Benjamin Tate was of a Leicestershire family but settled in Mitcham, Surrey. He partnered Price in many musical activities and in a letter to his friend Lord Haddington, Price described the state of music in London in a somewhat irreverent manner. Writing from London on 19 December 1741 he hoped that he and some of his friends would be able to help a composer named Fritz to find a publisher, but —

> they are such abominable Goths here ... they cannot bear anything but Handel, Courelli [*sic*], and Geminiani, which they are eternally playing ever and ever again at their concerts ... Tate and I are of a concert of gentlemen performers where Festing plays the first fiddle[13] ...

[10]*Literary Life and Select Works of Benjamin Stillingfleet,* "Character of Robert Price," II, 169–182.

[11]*ibid.,* 172 fn.

[12]*ibid.,* 160.

[13]Quoted in O. E. Deutsch, *Handel — A Documentary Biography,* London 1955, 528.

Lord Haddington, with his brother George Baillie, and their eccentric tutor, John Williamson, were also members of the Geneva company. Another aristocrat was Robert Neville Aldworth Neville, who broke off his studies at Oxford in 1739 in order to further them in Switzerland. The last important member of the company was Thomas Dampier, a former Scholar of Eton College and, since 1735, a Fellow of King's College, Cambridge.

For each of his Geneva friends Stillingfleet composed a complimentary ode, and together with Windham and Price compiled *An Account of the Glacieres or Ice Alps in Savoy* (1741). Price was responsible for the drawings, which recall the contemporary discovery of Alpine scenery as a new theme for artists by the water-colorist Alexander Cozens, and which point towards the "picturesque" ideas promoted by his son Uvedale.

Stillingfleet and Windham returned to England in 1743. Neville spent five winters in Geneva from 1739. Dampier was appointed Under-Master at Eton College in 1745. In 1746 Price married Sarah, sister of Daines Barrington, and in the following year his son Uvedale was born. It would appear, then, that Smith's acquaintance with the members of the "Common Room at Geneva" (as they termed it) developed in the years following his wife's death, and not as suggested by Coxe after the engagement with "the grandson of old Peter Waters" (i.e. Peter Walter).

This connection made Smith the beneficiary of one of the most unscrupulous financiers in England. Savaged by Pope in more than one poem, and by Swift and Charles Hanbury Williams, and providing the model for Henry Fielding's "Peter Pounce," Peter Walter's obsession with "this *per Cent* and that *per Year*" brought him great wealth and various public offices of influence. When he died in 1746 he was over eighty, and his grandson came into an inheritance reckoned to be worth some £300,000.

Out of this Smith obtained leisure. He returned to the composition of opera, composing *Issipile* in 1743. The libretto was from Metastasio, from whom Smith also took those for *Dario* (Rotterdam, 1746), *Il Ciro riconosciuto,* and *Artaserse,* on which he worked in Aix-en-Provence.

The call for help from Handel brought Smith back into the mainstream of English musical life. As editorial and administrative assistant, and associate director, he was invaluable. *Messiah* performances had become annual events at the Foundling Hospital and, like Handel, Smith became closely associated with this institution. On 15 April 1752, money for the payment of artists and other expenses was made over to Smith for him to distribute. Two years later he was appointed Organist of the Hospital and he continued in this office until 1770, when he resigned after a difference of opinion with the authorities concerning the engagement of artists. Although much incapacitated in his later years, Handel was nominally the director of the annual performances and his name was so advertised. In April 1759, at the last moment, Smith's name was substituted for that of Handel, who did, however, manage to attend the performances.

A month after Handel's death Smith delivered to the Hospital a copy of the score and a set of parts of *Messiah*, in accordance with Handel's wishes. The Foundling Hospital performances continued; so did the Lenten oratorio seasons at Covent Garden, which came under the joint control of Smith and John Stanley (who had been engaged as solo organist for the *Messiah* at the Foundling Hospital in 1759). This arrangement terminated with Smith's retirement to Bath in 1774, when he was replaced by Thomas Linley of that city.

The death of Handel marked another stage in Smith's career. As his influence had been mostly behind the scenes and he was generally respected for his modesty, it was in one way fitting that the *Life of Handel* that appeared in 1760 carried no acknowledgment to Smith. Stillingfleet put the facts as follows:

> The Life of Handel, published anonymously, but written by the Rev. Mr. Mainwaring, from material principally communicated by Mr. Smith.

To this he added how Mainwaring (who properly kept himself in ghostly reserve) was indebted to Robert Price, whose

> works display a profound knowledge of the rules of art, and his taste and discriminating judgement will appear from his comparison of the Italian and German music, which was published in the Life of Handel, and drawn up at the request of the ingenious author.[14]

After his marriage Price had maintained open house for his artistic, literary, and scientific friends. Among those most ready to travel out of London by the Radnor coach, and to get off at Yazor, were Stillingfleet and Smith, for whom the house at Foxley Hill was a Parnassian retreat. Among other activities Price translated (and abridged) Rameau's *Démonstrations du Prin-*

[14]See *Memoirs of the Life of the late George Frederic Handel* (1760), 165f., and references to Tartini, 175 fn. and 183 fn. (Stillingfleet's). *Principles and Power of Harmony* (1771) is an exposition of and commentary on the theories of Tartini, with some free-ranging observations by Stillingfleet.

cipe de l'harmonie, and prepared the libretto for Smith's *Judith.* He was civilized in some ways beyond his contemporaries and tireless in the prosecution of the public duties assumed to be the responsibility of a country gentleman. Smith approved his friend's humane approach to his duties as magistrate, for Price "declined, as much as possible, sending petty offenders to prison or to the house of correction, from the conviction that such places were too often the schools of vice."[15]

This view of custodial sentencing is strangely modern. But Price had his weaknesses:

> His friend Mr. Smith, who knew him scarcely less intimately than Mr. Stillingfleet, informed me that he was by nature choleric, and extremely irritable; but completely subdued this defect in his temper.[16]

The years in which Smith was frequently in the company of Price and Stillingfleet were musically productive. Between 1755 and 1758 *Six Suits [sic] for the Harpsichord* and *A Collection of Lessons for the Harpsichord* were published, and two sets of fugues assembled. But Smith was intent on following in the footsteps of his master and further demonstrating competence in the field of oratorio. Stillingfleet, like Price, was a willing accomplice. Smith began work on Stillingfleet's grandiose literary variation on Milton's *Paradise lost* at Tate's house in Surrey 1 December 1757 and completed his score at Foxley Hill on 29 July 1758. The work was dedicated to Mrs. Elizabeth Montagu, first of the "blue-stockings," who was esteemed the "first of women" in the circle that surrounded David Garrick, according to his and Smith's mutual friend James Clutterbuck.[17]

On 5 March 1760 Stillingfleet wrote to his old Geneva friend, Richard Neville:

> I am just now come from the Oratorio [at Covent Garden] being the second time of performance; there was a very good house, though not quite so full as the first, but more than was expected. The music was exceeding well received, without the least disturbance, and I imagine we shall have it a third time. But that, Smith will determine

[15]Stillingfleet, *op. cit.,* 176

[16]*ibid.,* 180 fn.

[17]Clutterbuck (see *Anecdotes* p. 47) was a Commissioner of the Land Tax and the Turnpike Tax; a collector of pictures, and also a friend of Thomas Gainsborough.

tomorrow, when he has seen the receipts. I had a thousand copies of the words printed, which were sold the first day, and more were wanted. To-day a second edition came out; but what number were sold, I know not.[18]

Isabella Young, Charlotte Brent, Giulia Frasi and John Beard all sang in this work. But in spite of the popularity of these soloists in oratorio in general, the response of the public did not warrant any further performance. Undeterred, Stillingfleet plowed on and presented his friend with four more works — only printed privately in 1760 — to set in oratorio style. These were *Joseph, David and Bathsheba, Moses and Zipporah,* and *Medea. Joseph,* however, was rejected as being unfit for the stage and the author decided not to fill it out "with the number of songs necessary to give it a proper length of time in performing" — an observation which provides a commentary on the piecemeal manner of writing oratorio libretti then prevailing. Of the other projects Smith took up *Medea* and wrote music for two acts, but then found that the general opinion was that this text was quite as "improper" as that of Joseph.

Composing oratorios was one way of achieving success in the theatre. Opera provided a second opportunity. There was a third way, through songs and incidental music (such as Arne had so brilliantly provided for Drury Lane) for plays. When the time appeared propitious, Smith explored this possibility also. Here he was assisted initially by his acquaintance with David Garrick, whose connection with Smith's circle of friends was ensured by his commitment (which became operative in 1761) to act as guardian to William Windham's son, after Windham's death, together with Stillingfleet and Dampier.

When he did undertake Garrick's commission to write music for a Drury Lane production, Smith enjoyed at least a limited success. Supposedly, the text for *The Fairies,* which was first performed on 3 February 1755, was concocted by Garrick himself from Shakespeare but this was never acknowledged to be the case by Garrick. This is not surprising. The work was a hastily contrived mish-mash in which — according to the score — "where Shakespeare has not supplied the Composer with Songs, he has taken them from Milton, Waller, Lansdown, Dryden, Hammond etc. and it is hoped they will not seem unnaturally introduced." The Prologue to *The Fairies* was written and spoken by Garrick, who nicely praised the composer,

---

[18]Stillingfleet, *op. cit.*

whose music, he said, contained the "sparks he caught from his great master's blaze."

Next year came an adaptation of *The Tempest,* given its premiere at Drury Lane on 16 February 1756. Of this, as of its predecessor, Thomas Arne's brother-in-law, Theophilus Cibber, strongly disapproved:

> The 'Midsummer Night's Dream' has been minced and fricaseed into a thing called 'The Fairies', 'The Winter's Tale' mammocked [*sic*] into a droll, and 'The Tempest' castrated into an opera ... Yet this sly Prince [i.e. Garrick] would insinuate that all this ill-usage of the Bard is owing, forsooth, to his love of him.[19]

These works were, of course, intended only as money-spinning entertainments. *The Fairies,* for instance, was meant

> to bring out two Italian singers, Signor Curioni and Signor Passerini, who had some twenty-seven songs: for [Garrick] hankered after these exotics, and always had his agents in foreign countries.[20]

Passerini sang in *The Fairies,* but Curioni, who had been engaged at the Haymarket in 1754, did not. On the fly-leaf of the score of *The Fairies* (G.240.a) in the British Library there is a pencil note added at a later stage in the history of this work.

> Dr. Burney says no English operas in which the Dialogue was carried in Recitative were crowned with full success except this opera which was set in 1755 and Artazerzes [*sic*] by Dr. Arne 1763. But the success of both was temporary and depended so much on the singers, Guadagni and Frase [*sic*] in the Arne and Tenducci, Miss Brent and Peretti in the other that they could never be called stock pieces, or indeed be performed again with any success by inferior singers ...

In 1760 Smith provided songs for a "musical entertainment" — *The Enchanter* for Drury Lane, and a further collaboration with Garrick was a setting of his "How cruelly fated is Woman to Woe" for inclusion in plays as and when required.

The most important event in Smith's personal life at this time was his second marriage — in 1760 or 1761 — to the widow of an old friend, Dr.

---

[19]Percy Fitzgerald, *The Life of David Garrick,* London 1868, 2nd edition 1899, 158
[20]*ibid.*

William Coxe, a well-known London physician.[21] For Smith this meant a complete change in his way of life, for Barbara Coxe was the mother of six young children. If this marked the beginning of a new chapter the death of King George II in 1760, of Price and Windham in 1761, and of Smith's father in 1763, marked the end of another. From his father he inherited all the priceless material which had been left to the older Smith in Handel's Will. This material it was that helped the two Smiths into immortality.

With the accession of George III — a notable Handelian — Smith (who lived in Dean Street, Soho) was brought into the royal household as instructor to the King's mother, Princess Augusta (widow of Frederick, Prince of Wales, who had once led the Bononcini faction against Handel's supporters). The attachment of George III to Handel's music and his appreciation of Smith's direction of the oratorios, and the affection dispensed by the Dowager Princess to the guardian of the ark and covenant of the Handel tradition, afforded Smith a competence as well as the pleasure of a cordial relationship with the royal family. The extraordinary generosity of Smith in acknowledging this relationship by making over his collection of Handel MSS to the monarch in due course is one of the epochal gestures in musical history.

Smith was not the first to suffer the fate that goes with a too close relationship with, and loyalty to, a creative genius of the first order. In spite of his attempts to escape from such constriction he was clearly marked as a Handelian. There was a row of unperformed oratorios (the music mostly taken from others of Smith's works) as well as *Nabal* and *Gideon* — stitched together from Handel by Thomas Morell and Smith for Covent Garden in 1764 and 1769 respectively — to testify to an imperishable sense of dedication. And there was the maintenance of the main tradition by singers of whom Smith approved. Among these were Frasi, Brent (after 1766, Mrs. Pinto), Guadagni, Guarducci, Tenducci (succeeding Guadagni about 1770), and Isabella Young.

[21]William Coxe was a graduate of Corpus Christi College, Cambridge (M.B. 1738, M.D. 1743). In 1748 he became a Fellow of the College of Physicians, of which he was Censor (1750 and 1755) and Harveian Orator (1753). He was physician to the Westminster Hospital (1750–57) and sometime "physician to the king's household." In 1741 Coxe married Barbara Clark at Somerset House Chapel. In 1747 the Coxes lived in Cork Street, Burlington Gardens, and from 1754 in Clarges Street. Coxe's death was listed in the *Gentleman's Magazine* 1760, 202, under 29 March, and he was described as "an eminent physician." (Information from the Royal College of Physicians where notes communicated by J.C. Smith were transferred in MS to the Library copy of W. Munk's *Roll of the College,* 1878, II, 166.)

Within this tradition, however, the brief reign of Elizabeth Linley caused shock waves which carried Handelian oratorio into a new phase, in which the English oratorio-singer established her, or his, authority. Elizabeth Linley came to London from Bath in 1769, bringing with her the reputation for skill and beauty that she had early acquired in concerts arranged by her father in the Assembly Rooms of her native city. She not only sang like an angel, but looked like one (she was Joshua Reynolds's model for St. Cecilia).

> When she appeared at the Oxford oratorios, grave dons and young
> gentlemen commoners were alike subdued. In London, where she
> sang at Covent Garden, in the Lent of 1773, the King himself is said
> to have been as much fascinated by her eyes and voice as by the
> music of his favourite Handel.[22]

In April 1773 Elizabeth married Richard Brinsley Sheridan under romantic circumstances and — apart from honoring an engagement at the Three Choirs Festival in the autumn of that year — retired from the profession. Smith, who had been saddened by the death of the Princess Augusta a year earlier, and now discouraged by the departure of the brightest oratorio star of all, decided that it was time for him to retire from the London scene. The place for a cultivated English gentleman to go was Bath, where all the refinements met together in a Palladian paradise whose spa waters offered the hope of long life.

Smith began his retirement in Bath in Old Park House in Brock Street, which had been built according to the designs of John Wood junior in 1764. Here Smith and his wife lived with her daughter Emilia, who maintained a school for girls. Since Smith himself seems to have continued to teach, it is probable that the girls of his step-daughter's school were the beneficiaries of his experience. Barbara Smith died on 10 May 1786, after which Smith moved to 18 Bennet Street on the other side of the Circus.

In this brilliant era in the history of Bath its music was dominated by the engaging personality of Venanzio Rauzzini — an Italian castrato who came to London in 1774 and to Bath three years later. Rauzzini came to a place where the name of Handel was revered and where regular performances of his music had taken place over many years. The tradition had been established by Thomas Chilcot, the Abbey Organist to whose elegant Shakespeare songs Handel was a Subscriber, Thomas Linley, and Alexander Herschel. The

---

[22]Quoted by W. Clark Russell in *Representative Actors,* London n.d., 224, from C.R. Leslie, *Life and Times of Joshua Reynolds,* London 1865, 2 vols.

brother of William Herschel, Alexander was a cellist, and he took it on himself to arrange for Handel oratorio performances in the fashionable Octagon Proprietary Chapel in Milsom Street. With the coming of Rauzzini, advertisements for musical events became more alluring. The Subscription Concerts arranged by Rauzzini, according to the *Bath Journal,* were "such as to render that elegant branch of the Amusement of this Place, superior to any in the Kindgom." There was a fashionable Catch Club, and an equally fashionable Harmonic Society, over which Dr. Henry Harington — physician and composer, and Subscriber to the *Anecdotes* — presided. Each Passion week the decencies were maintained under Rauzzini's regimen by a series of "Evening Concerts" in the "New Room." These comprised excerpts from Handel's oratorios and employed as many as 150 performers. As elsewhere in Britain, *Messiah* was held in sanctified reserve for charity occasions and the Abbey Church; as, for example, "for the emolument of the Children of the Sunday Schools" on 12 April 1794. During this performance Handel's

> 2nd Organ Concerto [was] given between the parts of the Oratorio by Mr. Field, who tho' a very young man is too well known for his ability to need any panegyric.

This reference in the *Bath Journal* was to Thomas Field — soon to be appointed Organist of Bath Abbey — who, at the age of seventeen, was already well established in the City as a virtuoso performer. Field is also among those who subscribed to the *Anecdotes.*

On 12 October 1795 the *Bath Journal* carried this brief notice:

> Saturday died in Upper Church-street John Christopher Smith, Esq., aged 83 years, who was the pupil, assistant and friend of the immortal Handel, and his successor in conducting the oratorios.

Smith was buried in the churchyard of the eighteenth-century church of St. Swithin, Walcot, in Bath, where in due course Jane Austen's father and Fanny Burney were to be interred. Smith's Will, signed on 13 May 1786 and witnessed by William Melmoth, designated benefactions as follows: his books in English — apart from those of a theological nature — as well as a ring and various pictures to Peter Coxe[23]; the portrait of Handel by Denner to William Coxe, who shared the remaining pictures with his brother Ed-

---

[23]Peter Coxe was a friend of Sir John Soane and a minor poet, whose principal work was *The Social Day: a Poem in four Cantos,* London 1823.

ward[24]; theological works and a gold watch to George Coxe[25]; music books and a snuff-box with a picture of her son Thomas on the lid to Lady Rivers, née Martha Coxe[26]; and books in French — likely to be of value to a teacher — as well as household effects to Emilia Coxe with whom Smith had spent most of his last years.

William Melmoth, who witnessed the Will, was a notable figure in the intellectual life of Bath. Occupied — rather lightly one would suppose in Bath — as a Commissioner of Bankrupts, his main interests were in scholarship and in *belles lettres*. He had been a friend of William Coxe's father — as is indicated on p. 52 of the *Anecdotes* — and the friendship was extended to the younger William, whose *Travels in Switzerland* (1789) was addressed to Melmoth in the then-favored form of "letters."[27]

[24]Art connoisseur; works from his collection were auctioned in 1807 at the instance of Peter Coxe.

[25]George Coxe, educated at Winchester and Eton Colleges and Cambridge University, is commemorated by a tablet on the north wall of the church of St. Michael in the Soke, Winchester. This records that he was for more than thirty years Rector of that church, and that he died on 30 July 1844, aged 87. His wife had died a year earlier, aged 90. A neighboring tablet is a tribute to George's sister Emaelia Henrietta Coxe (who seems therefore to have left Bath to live with her brother), who died on 30 November 1841 in her 95th year.

[26]Martha Coxe married Rev. Sir Peter Rivers Bart., Prebendary of Winchester, in 1768. He died in 1790. The snuff-box had been left to him but passed to his widow. Their son Thomas died in 1805. He was succeeded in the baronetcy by his brother James, who, however, died as the consequence of an accident with a fowling-piece in the same year. Rev. Sir Henry, the fourth son (William, the third, died in 1794), like his uncle William was a Steward of the Sons of the Clergy. The Denner portrait of Handel seems to have passed from William Coxe to his brother Peter, who collected works by Denner, and then to Lady Rivers, from whom it came to the Sacred Harmonic Society and finally to the National Portrait Gallery. Lady Rivers died c. 1835. There are memorial stones to numerous members of the Rivers family in the north aisle of Winchester Cathedral. Adjacent to them is one of a Mrs. Hannah Coxe, Relict of Samuel Coxe, of Stoke Newington [London]. She died on 15 August 1775, aged 06. It seems not unlikely that Samuel Coxe had been a brother of William Coxe Sr.

[27]There are some eleven Letters addressed to Philotes in *Fitzosborne's Letters*, dated between 1735 and 1744 (some are without date), on such matters as portrait painting, travel, cruelty to insects, Robert Boyle's moderation in respect to scientific speculation, spa life in Tunbridge, and some personal matters. Letter XVII, dated 1 February 1738, refers to Philotes' marriage and to Aspasia. That date is incompatible with the information said to have come from Smith and inlcuded in Munk's *Roll* (see note 21 above)

In Letter XXXV, addressed to "Cleora" there is a reference which might appear to have some relevance to Smith and Lockman:

> ... As I imagined Tereminta would, by this time, be with you, I had a view to her harpsichord in the composition, and I desire you would let her know, I hope she will shew me, at my return, to what advantage the most ordinary numbers will appear, when judiciously accompanied with a fine voice and instrument.

There follows the words for three airs, a recitative, and two choruses for an *Ode for Music*, written by Melmoth.

William Coxe junior was a characteristic figure of his age, and his smooth progress — as the comfortable life-style of his brothers and sisters — testifies to the zeal with which Smith had carried out the injunction he had received from Dr. Coxe, to care for his family. William was educated at Eton College and King's College, Cambridge, of which he became a Fellow. During his time in Cambridge the Organist of King's College was John Randall — also Professor of Music in the University — who as a Chapel Royal chorister had sung in Handel's *Esther* when it was revived in 1732. After ordination Coxe enjoyed the patronage of the great, being given sinecure tutorships and comfortable and undemanding ecclesiastical appointments. In his *Travels in Switzerland* he described himself as "Rector of Bemerton; Member of the Imperial Oeconomical Society at St. Petersburgh, of the Royal Academy of Sciences at Copenhagen, and Chaplain to His Grace the Duke of Marlborough." Bemerton, famous because George Herbert had once been its Vicar, was near Salisbury, of which Coxe became Archdeacon in 1804. In the following year he was appointed one of the "Stewards of the Sons of the Clergy," and in 1807 he preached the Sermon at the annual Service in St. Paul's Cathedral. In the course of this he said that,

> In science and in art the members of the Church [of England] have always held an eminent place among their contemporaries.

He himself was determined also to hold an eminent place, at least in the field of letters. He was well-read, industrious, well connected socially, and enthusiastic — an admirable camp-follower in the line of Price, Windham, Neville, and Dampier, but more energetic than any of them. He was, indeed, an obsessive writer, whose works covered a wide range of human affairs. The *Anecdotes* he saw as an act of piety. He respected his step-father and revered the great Handel, and if Mainwaring and — by now — Burney had exploited Smith's notes, directly and indirectly, and thereby accumulated credit, Coxe was determined that credit should also go to Smith. More than this, any profits from the compilation of the *Anecdotes* should go to surviving members of the Smith family, presumably John Christopher's nephews and nieces.

A considerable body of well-known persons supported Coxe's enterprise. Some names recalled the past, some pointed to the future, and some did both. John Adolphus, lawyer and politician, was the grandson of Frederick the Great's physician, and he assisted Coxe in compiling the *Memoirs of Sir Robert Walpole*. John Julius Angerstein, merchant and philanthropist, assembled a collection of pictures that was the basis of the National Gallery; like Coxe he was a Steward of the Sons of the Clergy. Lord Braybrooke was a son of Richard Neville, of the Genevan "Common Room." Bishop Thomas Dampier was also the son of a member of that company. Samuel Whitbread, a celebrated politician, had once been under Coxe's tutelage during his statutory European tour. Lord Fitzwilliam was the founder of the Museum at Cambridge, where there is much material relating to Handel which conceivably came to him direct from Smith. Various members of the Tate family — including Benjamin junior — and a Mrs Waters (*sic*) also recall old associations. But of all the Subscribers to the *Anecdotes* no name is more significant than that of Uvedale Price.

In his *Essays on the Picturesque* (1798) Price proceeded from the standpoint of his father. He was widely cultured, a responsible citizen, a good host, and an excellent writer. In an elegant passage he demonstrates, with reference to Handel, that linkage of eras otherwise illustrated by the outline of Smith's career:

> If ever there was a truly great and original genius in any art, Handel was that genius in music; and yet, what may seem no slight paradox, there never was a greater plagiary. He seized without scruple or concealment, whatever suited his purpose. But as those sweets which the bee steals from a thousand flowers, by passing through its little laboratory, are converted into a substance peculiar to itself, and which no other art can effect, — so, whatever Handel stole, by passing through the powerful laboratory of his mind, and mixing with his ideas, became as much his own as if he had been the inventor. Like the bee, too, by his manner of working, he often gave to what was unnoticed in its original situation, something of high and exquisite flavour. To Handel might well be applied, what Boileau, with more truth than modesty, says of himself — Et même en imitant toujours originel.[28]

Appearing in 1799 the *Anecdotes* had a reassuring effect, and their influence continued certainly throughout the nineteenth century. The image of Handel, created so soon after his death, was ratified. In spite of the changes

[28]Uvedale Price, "Essay on Decorations," in *Essays on the Picturesque as compared with the Sublime and the Beautiful*, Hereford 1798, II, 196.

wrought in an age of technological and social upheaval, the great master — a national hero — was felt beatifically to preside over human affairs from an Olympian eminence. The last three pages of the *Anecdotes* are painted by Coxe with supreme confidence and a broad brush in the genial tinctures of comfortable Anglicanism. Coxe is rather grander in manner than John Mainwaring[29]; but he worked from somewhat different premises.

Mainwaring's place in the Handelian field is difficult to explain, but there is one clue, perhaps, as to his reason for performing an emergency operation as biographer extraordinary. A prominent member of a university community, he objected to too much specialism, criticizing particularly the stress laid on mathematics at Cambridge. It was his own objective "to establish merit on a *broader* as well as a *sounder* basis."[30] In particular, this would naturally lead to the ranking of a great creative musician — whose powers in the field of religion were so manifest — as a great man. This much appears to be the message from the last page of the *Life of Handel*. Coxe, apart from wishing to satisfy his apparent ambition to conquer all spheres of learning, was inspired by a determination to do justice to his stepfather, and to remind the world that what appeared to the world as the authentic image of Handel was in some measure due to John Christopher Smith. If the one was indisputably great, he would show how the other was, beyond doubt, good.

However, in the closing years of the eighteenth century (Coxe was authoritative on European affairs) it was clear that even the reputation of Handel was likely to be subject to change. Coxe was mindful of the consequences of the great Westminster Abbey Commemoration of 1784 — to which his stepfather had been invited but which he felt unable to attend — and he shows how the occasion seemed to have given new vigor to old truths. The dominant philosophic theme of Coxe is the "majesty" of Handel, and as Pope had once spoken of this (in his youth Smith had the temerity to take up the point with him) so now Coxe brings in the younger supportive voices of William Mason and Mark Akenside. In his Advertisement Coxe acknowledges the authority of Mainwaring, Burney and Hawkins, but the inclusion of "original Anecdotes ... derived from unquestionable authority" points back to the prime source of knowledge of Handel in England.

[29]During a continental tour with Samuel Whitbread in 1785–1786 Coxe met Mainwaring in Rome.

[30]Edward Miller, *Portrait of a College: A History of the College of Saint John the Evangelist Cambridge,* Cambridge 1961, 62.

There are two types of anecdote in Coxe: the one representing Smith's recollections of information derived from his father, from Handel himself, or from others in the circle of first-hand acquaintance; the other coming directly from Smith. There is a relationship between the two, particularly in the dissemination of inaccuracy. One of the first to recognize and to deplore palpable inaccuracies in Mainwaring (due to Mainwaring's assumption that what he had from Smith was correct) was Johann Mattheson, as Burney points out in the *Commemoration*.[31]

For such inaccuracies there were reasons. In the first place items retrieved from the recesses of memory and transferred to another memory bank, to be withdrawn after the passage of much time and many vicissitudes and to be given literary shape, are likely to be more colorful at the end than at the beginning. Then there is the matter of intention. Coxe draws attention to particular circumstances: it was singularly appropriate that a great musician should arrive in England when he did, to hymn the glories of a nation "at this time no less successful in war than in the arts of peace." That provided the setting for a hero. But against the hero — who must have the dragon in order to play St. George — there had to be an anti-hero.

Reinhardt Keiser was effectively set up for this role, and the damage done to his reputation by Smith (was he put up to it by Handel?) was not repaired for two centuries. He was but the first of many whose personal qualities and/or musical talents were subject to often intemperate comment from Handel zealots. Some of this is apparent in the *Anecdotes*. But sometimes, when the author is off guard, some truths come through with especial force. Particularly, there is a poignant emphasis on the loneliness of Handel. His love affairs disappear into the hinterland of emotion, and in middle age the tensions came to a climax in the mental disturbances which caused Handel to seek therapy in Aix-la-Chapelle in 1737. (Coxe does not directly relate this.) There is one chilling sentence in the *Anecdotes*: "Handel contracted few intimacies, and when his early friends died, he was not solicitous of acquiring new ones."

There are one or two persons whose involvement with Handel's career would seem to be endorsed by the Smith connection. Kielmansegge's part in

---

[31]See p. 11: Mattheson accused Mainwaring "not only of violating geography, chronology, and history, but of a wilful misrepresentation of facts" in regard to the supposed quarrel between Handel and Mattheson. Burney, however, had previously demolished Mattheson as "a vain and pompous man, whose first wish in all his writings was to impress the reader with due reverence for his own abilities and importance."

the restoration to favor of Handel at the court of George I may well have come to Smith by way of Lady Mary Howe, who was Kielmansegge's daughter. The interest of Frederick the Great of Prussia (twice mentioned in the *Anecdotes*), not otherwise remarked by early biographers and regarded as unlikely by some later ones, is apparently supported by a notice — sent from Haarlem on 22 September 1740 — in the *Hamburger Relations-Courier* which, having described Handel's activities in Holland, ends, "Man sagt, dass vorbemeldeter Hr. Hendel sich nach Berlin zu begeben entschlossen sey." Handel, in short, purportedly intended to go to Berlin. And the King of Prussia at the time was reconstituting the court musical establishment.

In the more direct testimony concerning Smith's own early career there are some surprising gaps. What, one is entitled to ask, did all those celebrities gathered together at Arbuthnot's talk about? The omission is the more strange in view of Smith's preference for men of faculties other than that of music. Here there are homely references to Pepusch and Roseingrave, and a nice passing mention of William Topham, the pugilistic composer of a set of flute sonatas published by John Walsh.

Smith associated with men of influence — while himself wielding none — and with poets and painters (it was a mark of his respectability that he was painted by Zoffany), divines and scholars. With none of these did he compete, and from the evidence available it is clear that his support for many of their projects was a beneficent factor. But he had set out to be a composer. Here too his intermediary function has more significance than his immediate creative activity. By no stretch of the imagination can he be described as other than a "minor" composer — which status is underwritten by Coxe's appended selection of pieces "never before published" in the *Anecdotes*.

Smith's amiability is generally reflected in his compositions. His keyboard works lay well within the capacity of well-bred young ladies who took Stillingfleet's advice and dedicated themselves to three years of music study. In energy and robustness of statement they are well behind the comparable works of his teacher, Roseingrave, and in spaciousness and constructive development not to be compared with those of Handel. There was a market for teaching material and Smith's Lessons and Sonatas served a useful, if limited, purpose within this market.

The influence of da capo aria in general conditioned Smith to challenge the ambivalence of English taste with works couched in the fashionable *lingua italiana* of the first half of the eighteenth century. To this fashion his most considerable tribute was *Issipile,* comprising 28 da capo arias — and a conventional finale in the form of a bouncing *Coro* in ⅜ time. In the grand oratorio manner Smith's essays were to be compared neither with Handel's works of this order nor with the masterly large-scale anthems of Croft, Greene, and others. With Smith one fatal defect was a frequent incompatibility between verbal accentuation and rhythmic structure, while concessions to virtuoso singers often led to coloratura passages that were merely obstructive.

Smith, however, has a special place in that he was near the center of the complex argument (of which the echoes carried over for a very long time) concerning the provision of a form of music drama in England that was both aesthetically convincing and also meaningful. John Lockman was but one of a group which interested itself in the reform of music drama towards a genuine English opera. Lockman's introductory essay in the word-book of *Rosalinda* indicates the condition from which it was felt opera should be raised.

> The Badness of most of the English Versions of the *Italian* Operas, as well as of the Originals, seemed to give the Town a Contempt for all musical Poems in general; and this, joined to the arbitrary Behaviour of some of the Composers, who either were ignorant of the genuine Beauties of a theatrical Poem, or determined to sacrifice 'em, whenever they thought proper, to the Charm of Sound, made so strong an Impression on Authors of Capacity, that none of 'em cared to employ their Talents that Way . . .

At a later point Lockman acknowledged that he was "greatly obliged on many Accounts to some of the ablest" of composers — including, presumably, J.C. Smith, whose earlier works in what was considered a novel Italo-English style were an indication of new musical paths rather than exceptional in their own right. The truth is that Smith was not a dramatic composer.

In the popular field of Garrick-Shakespeare, Smith's talents appear as more apposite. Occasional inelegant accidents of accentuation and complex melodic roulades — parodies of Handel — are sometimes set off by an agreeable picturesqueness. The overtures to *The Fairies, The Tempest,* and *The Enchanter* are brisk and to the point. His instrumental incidental music — the Hornpipe of *The Tempest* and the Dead March of *The Enchanter,* for example — is usually economical and effective. In respect of vocal numbers Smith was too indulgent to his singers' reputations. He was able to engage the best — and they made their own demands. Hence the frequent overloading of melodic line with decorative features that merely held up the flow. On the other hand Smith could compel an attentive ear with his adroit use of formula; for instance, the turgid chromatics and tonal changes of "Arise, ye subterranean winds" and the bell effects of pizzicato strings for "Full fathom five" in *The Tempest*; the flamboyant opening (the idea borrowed from Handel's Polyphemus music) of Moroc's "I burn" in *The Enchanter,* and the contrasting artlessness of "When Youthful Charms fly Phoebus' Arms" in the same work.

In Smith the composer there is to be found a resolute, less than inspired, artificer with the attributes of a provincial *Kapellmeister.* Perhaps this is not altogether surprising: behind John Christopher Smith lay centuries of German musical tradition.

PERCY M. YOUNG
Wolverhampton, England
April 1979

BIBLIOGRAPHY

COXE, WILLIAM: *A Sermon preached at the Anniversary Meeting of the Sons of the Clergy, 14 May 1807,* London 1808

———: *A Historical Tour through Monmouthshire,* second edition, Brecon 1904; with "Memoir of the Author" and Frontispiece — "William Coxe M.A., Archdeacon of Wilts., from the original picture by Sir W. Beechey R.A."

———: (ed.) *Literary Life and Select Works of Benjamin Stillingfleet,* London 1801, 3 vols.

DEAN, WINTON: "Charles Jennens' Marginalia to Mainwaring's Life of Handel," *Music and Letters* 53, no. 3, 1972

DRUMMOND, PIPPA: "The Royal Society of Musicians in the Eighteenth Century," *Music and Letters* 59, no. 3, 1978

FITZGERALD, PERCY: *The Life of David Garrick,* London 1868, second edition 1899

FLESSA, ERNST: *Ombra mai fu ... Die Händel-Chronik des Johann Christoph Smith,* Biberach an der Riss, 1958

GARRICK, DAVID: *Private Correspondence of,* London 1831, 2 vols.

HALL, JAMES S.: "John Christopher Smith, Handel's Friend and Secretary," *Musical Times,* March 1955

———: "John Christopher Smith: his Residence in London," *Händel-Jahrbuch* 1957, Leipzig 1957

———: "John Christopher Smith, 1712–1795," *Händel-Jahrbuch* 1964–65

HUMPHRIES, CHARLES AND SMITH, WILLIAM C.: *Music Publishing in the British Isles,* London 1954

MANN, ALFRED: "Eine Kompositionslehre von Händel," *Händel-Jahrbuch* 1964–65

MATTHEWS,BETTY: "Unpublished Letters concerning Handel," *Music and Letters,* 40, no. 3, 1959

McCREDIE, ANDREW D.: "Über John Christopher Smith", Programme book of Göttingen Handel Festival, Göttingen 1961

MELMOTH, WILLIAM: *Fitzosborne's Letters,* Harrison's Edition, London 1787

NICHOLS, R.H. AND WRAY, F.A.: *The History of the Foundling Hospital,* London 1935

SASSE, KONRAD: "Neue Daten zu Johann Christoph Schmidt," *Händel-Jahrbuch* 1957

SMITH, WILLIAM C.: "More Handeliana", *Music and Letters* 34, no. 1, 1953

[STILLINGFLEET, BENJAMIN]: *Principles and Power of Harmony,* London 1771

WORKS BY JOHN CHRISTOPHER SMITH

KEYBOARD

Suites de Pieces, 1732;
Second Set, c. 1735
Lessons, Op. 3, c. 1755
Lessons, Op. 4, c. 1757
Sonatas, 1763
Unpublished fugues.
   (Harpsichord pieces by J.C.
     Smith and others copied by
     Charles Burney in Chester in
     1744, BL, ADD MS 39957)

CANTATAS, SONGS, ETC.

The mourning Muse of Alexis, J.
   Arbuthnot (?), c. 1729
Daphne, A. Pope, 1744
Thamesis, Isis and Proteus,
   c. 1751 (?)
"How cruelly fated is Woman to
Woe," in *Thalia, a Collection of
Six Favourite Songs,*
occasionally introduced in
Several Dramatic Performances
at the Theatre Royal in Drury
Lane, the Words by David
Garrick Esq., 1767.

ORATORIO STYLE & CHORAL

*David's Lamentation over Saul
   and Jonathan*, J. Lockman,
   1738
Paradise Lost, B. Stillingfleet,
   1758
Judith, R. Price, c. 1760
Rebecca, author of text not known,
   1761
The Feast of Darius, author of text
   not known, music borrowed
   from *Dario*, c. 1761

Nabal, T. Morell, from Handel,
  recits by Smith, 1764
Jehosaphat, author of text not
  known, 1764
Gideon, T. Morell, from Handel,
  1769
The Foundling Hymn, 1763
*Funeral Service for the Dowager
  Princess Augusta of Wales,*
  1772.

OPERA, SERENADE, & OTHER
DRAMATIC MUSIC

Teraminta, H. Carey, 1732
Ulysses, S. Humphreys, 1733
Rosalinda, J. Lockman, music
  lost, 1740
Issipile, Metastasio, 1743
Il Ciro riconosciuto, Metastasio,
  1746
Dario, Metastasio, music lost,
  1746
Artaserse, Metastasio, 1748
Medea, B. Stillingfleet,
  unfinished, c. 1760.

The Seasons, author of text
  unknown, 1740.

The Fairies, D. Garrick after
  Shakespeare, 1755
The Tempest, D. Garrick after
  Shakespeare, 1756
The Enchanter, D. Garrick, 1760.
  Overtures to *The Fairies, The
  Tempest,* and *The Enchanter*
  published with works by Abel
  and Arne in *Six Favourite
  Overtures for Violins,
  Hoboys, and French Horns
  etc.,* J. Walsh, 1760.

The items given at the end of
  the *Anecdotes* were
  separately issued as *Select
  Pieces of Music by The late
  John Christopher Smith never
  before publish'd:* London,
  Birchall, New Bond Street.

ANECDOTES

OF

GEORGE FREDERICK HANDEL,

AND

JOHN CHRISTOPHER SMITH.

GEORGE FREDERICK HANDEL,

From an Original Picture Painted by Denner.

Published May 1.1799, by Cadell & Davies, Strand.

ANECDOTES

OF

GEORGE FREDERICK HANDEL,

AND

JOHN CHRISTOPHER SMITH.

———

WITH

SELECT PIECES OF MUSIC,

COMPOSED

BY J. C. SMITH,

NEVER BEFORE PUBLISHED.

———

LONDON:

PRINTED BY W. BULMER AND CO.

SOLD BY CADELL AND DAVIES, STRAND; E. HARDING, PALL-MALL;

BIRCHALL, MUSIC-SELLER, BOND-STREET; AND

J. EATON, SALISBURY.

1799.

TO

MR. PETER COXE,

IN GRATITUDE,

AS WELL FOR VARIOUS

COMMUNICATIONS AND JUDICIOUS REMARKS,

AS FOR HIS STRENUOUS EXERTIONS

IN PROMOTING THE SUBSCRIPTION,

AND AS

A MEMORIAL OF PRIVATE FRIENDSHIP,

THESE ANECDOTES

ARE INSCRIBED.

Bemerton,
April 20, 1799.

ADVERTISEMENT.

In submitting to the Public, Anecdotes of Handel, some apology may be expected, as his Life has been already given in numerous productions. The motives which gave rise to this attempt, must plead an excuse. The profits of this Publication being appropriated to the use of the Relations of Mr. Smith, whose Memoirs are now first presented to the world.

For the Memoirs of Handel, the best printed accounts have been consulted. " The Memoirs of the Life of George Frederick Handel, 8vo. 1760," which were written under the inspection of Mr. Smith;" " Sir John Hawkins's History of Music:"—" an Account of the Musical Performances in Commemoration of Handel;" " the present State of Music in Germany and the Netherlands;" and, " the History of Music;" all by Dr. Burney. Some original Anecdotes are interspersed, derived from unquestionable authority.

The Portrait of Handel is engraven from an original picture painted by Denner, in 1736 or 1737, which Handel gave to Mr. Smith; who left it to his son in law, the Rev. William Coxe, in whose possession it now remains. The Portrait of Mr. Smith is engraven from a picture by Zoffani, now in the possession of Mr. Peter Coxe.

LIST OF SUBSCRIBERS.

The Names of the Subscribers for fine Paper Copies are marked with.

Adolphus, Mr.
Anderson, John, Esq.
* Angerstein, John Julius, Esq.
Astle, Thomas, Esq. Keeper of the Re-
cords, Tower

Bagwill, John, Esq.
* Balfour, Blaney, Esq.
Balfour, Mrs.
Balfour, Miss
Barnes, Rev. F. Master of Peter House,
Cambridge
* Barnes, John, Esq.
* Baronneau, Francis, Esq.
* Barrington, Hon. Daines, 5 Copies
* Barrington, Hon. Admiral
* Bath and Wells, the Lord Bishop of
Beatniffe, Mr.
* Beckingham, Rev. John Charles
Bell, William, Esq.
Bentham, Miss, Oxford.
Birchall, Mr. Music-seller, Bond-street,
18 Copies
Bird, William, Esq.
* Blaney, Rev. Dr. Christ's Ch. Oxford
Bowdon, William, Esq.
* Braybrook, Lord, 5 Copies
Bremner, Mr. Bookseller, 3 Copies.
Brogham, Rev. John
* Brooksbank, Mrs. 5 Copies
Brooke, Rev. Richard
* Bryant, Jacob, Esq.
* Bryan, Michael, Esq.
Bull, Robert, Esq.

Bureau, James, Esq.
Burrell, Mr. Charles
Burrows, Capt. Thomas

* Cadell and Davies, Messrs. 10 Copies
* Call, Lady
* Call, Miss
Callender, Henry, Esq.
* Cancellor, John, Esq.
Carr, Rev. Mr.
* Chalmers, George, Esq.
Chalmers, Charles, Esq.
* Chaloner, George, Esq.
Champion, Alexander, Esq.
Champion, Benjamin, Esq.
Chard, Mr. Winchester
Christie, Robert, Esq.
Clinton, Hon. Mrs.
Cock, Mr.
Cole, Benjamin, Esq.
Colkett, ———, Esq.
Collier, J. P. Esq.
Combe, Boyce, Esq.
Cotton, Mrs. S. Bath
* Coxe, Rev. William, 5 Copies
* Coxe, Edward, Esq. 5 Copies
* Coxe, Peter, Esq. 5 Copies
* Coxe, Rev. George, 5 Copies
* Coxe, Mrs. Emilia, 5 Copies
Crokatt, Henry, Esq.
Crotch, Mr. Oxford
Crowl, C. Esq.
Cure, Capel, Esq.
* Curtis, Rev. J. A. Vicar of Bitton

b

* Dampier, Rev. Dr. Dean of Rochester
  Dance, Rev. Thomas, Downton
* D'Aranda, Mrs. Putney
  Davison, Craufurd, Esq.
  Dean, John, Esq.
* De la Cour, William, Esq.
  Delap, Samuel, Esq.
  Delap, Mrs.
  Delap, Miss Mary Ann
  Dinsley, Mr. William
  Du Bois, C. H. Esq.
* Durham, the Hon. and Right Rev. the
  Lord Bishop of, 2 Copies

  Easton, Mr. Bookseller, Salisbury, 14
  Copies
* Egremont, the Earl of, 5 Copies
  Erwin, Edward, Esq.
* Eyre, the Rev. Dr. Canon of Sarum.

* Faulder, Mr Bookseller, 7 Copies
* Fawkner, William, Esq.
  Field, Mr. Organist, Bath.
  Fisher, Rev. Dr. Canon of Windsor
* Fitzwilliam, Lord Viscount, 4 Copies
  Forster, Rev. Dr. Canon of Windsor
  Forster, Rev. Dr. Norwich
  Forsyth, James, Esq.
  Foster, Mr. Charles
  Fraser, William, Esq.
* Freeling, Francis, Esq. Secretary to the
  Post Masters General

* Gardner, Mr. William, 2 Copies
  Gawen, Miss Eliza
* Gillbee, William, Esq.
  Gillon, John, Esq.
* Goldsworthy, Lieutenant General, 2
  Copies
  Golightly, William, Esq.
* Gregg, Thomas, Esq.
* Grey de Wilton, Lord

* Harding, Mr. E. No. 98, Pall-Mall,
  19 Copies
* Hardwicke, Earl of, 2 Copies
  Harrington, Dr.
  Harris, Miss Louisa
  Hartley, Mrs. M. Bath,
  Henslow, Mrs. Chatham Yard
  Hetley, Rev. H. Wilton
  Hibbut, Mr. Fellow of King's College,
  Cambridge
  Hippuff, Charles, Esq.
* Hoare, Sir R. C. Bart. 2 Copies
* Holroyd, Mrs. Bath, 5 Copies
  Horden, Mr. Peterborough
* Humphreys, Mrs. Bath

* Ingles, Rev. Henry
  Irving, John, Esq.
  Jacob, Rev. Mr. Salisbury
  Jennings, John, Esq.

* Keene, Benjamin, Esq.
  King's Library
  King's College Library
  Kirwan, Anthony, Esq.

* Law, Edward, Esq.
* Le Blanc, Simon, Esq. 5 Copies
  Leckie, George, Esq.
* Leeds, Duke of, 2 Copies
* Leigh, John, Esq. Bath
* Leycester, Hugh, Esq. 5 Copies
  Lyon, George, Esq.

  Maddison, John, Esq.
  Mainwaring, Rev. Mr.
* Malmesbury, Lord, 2 Copies
* Maltby, Miss
  Maule, Rev. Mr.
  Melmoth, Mrs.
  Meyer, John, Esq. Clapham, 3 Copies
  Meyer, John, Esq. M. D.
  Middleton, Rev. T. F.

M'Intosh, John, Esq.
Mitchell, William, Esq.
Montgomery, Miss
Montgomery, Miss Mary
Morton, Charles, Esq.
* Moss, Rev. C. D. D. Canon Residentiary of St. Paul's
Musgrave, Sir William, Bart.

* Napier, Lady
* Nesbitt, John, Esq. M. P.
Newcastle, Duchess of
* Newton, Francis, Esq.
Nichols, Mr. Printer, 2 Copies
Nicol, Mr. Bookseller, Pall-Mall
Nugent, Miss
Nugent, Miss Henrietta

Ogden, Mrs. Salisbury
Ogle, William Meade, Esq.
Ord, Mrs.

* Pack, Miss, Prestwould, near Loughborough, Leicestershire, 5 Copies
Parry, Thomas, Esq.
Parsons, Miss, Oxford
* Payne, Mr. Bookseller, 8 Copies
* Peachy, Hon. John
* Pembroke, Countess of, 5 Copies
* Pembroke, the Earl of, 5 Copies
* Pennant, Thomas, Esq.
Pettiward, Roger, Esq.
Philpott, Mr. Bath
Pim, William, Esq.
* Pillans, W. C. Esq.
* Platt, John, Esq.
* Porter, William, Esq.
Potts, James, Esq.
* Pretyman, Rev. Dr. Prebendary of Norwich.
* Price, Uvedale, Esq. 5 Copies
* Price, Rev. Robert, D. D. Prebendary of Durham, 5 Copies
* Price, William, Esq. 5 Copies
Puget, Mrs.

* Pusey, Hon. Philip, 10 Copies

* Quin, Mrs. Bath

Ravenhill, John, Esq.
Rivaz, V. F. Esq.
* Rivers, Lady, Winchester, 5 Copies
* Rivers, Sir Thomas, Bart. 5 Copies
* Rivers, James, Esq.
* Rivers, Miss
* Roberts, Thomas, Esq.
Robinson, Hon. Mrs.
* Robson, Mr. Bookseller, 2 Copies
Rogers, Joseph, Esq.
* Roxburgh, Duke of, 2 Copies
Rudge, Miss

* Salisbury, the Lord Bishop of
* Scudamore, Mrs. A. Hereford, 5 Copies
Shedden, Robert, Esq.
Shee, George, Esq.
Shee, Martin Arthur. Esq. A. R. A.
Sheffield, Lord
Shield, William, Esq.
Skipsey, William, Esq. R. N.
* Smith, Sir John, Bart.
Sneyd, Rev. William
Sneyd, Rev. Thomas, Ballyborough
Sneyd, Nathaniel, Esq.
Spear, Miss, Ballyborough
Steell, Robert, Esq.
* Steers, J. W. Esq
* Steers, Charles, Esq. 2 Copies
* Steers, Edward, Esq.
Stepple, Henry, Esq.
Still, Robert, Esq.
Still, Rev. John
Stokes, John, Esq.
Story, Rev. Joseph
Story, Rev. Edward
Story, Miss Anna
* Sumner, Rev. Dr. Provost of King's College, Cambridge, 2 Copies
Sumner, Rev. Mr. Fellow of King's College, Cambridge

Swale, John, Esq.

Swale, Mrs. C.

Swale, Miss F.

* Tate, George, Esq. 2 Copies
* Tate, Mrs. Grosvenor Place, 2 Copies
* Tate, Miss, 2 Copies
* Tate, Rev. Benjamin

Tatlow, Miss Mary

Tatlow, Miss Charlotte

Tatlow, Master John

* Thompson, Henry, Esq.

Thurlow, Miss

* Tighe, R. S. Esq.

Turner, Rev. J. D. D. Dean of Norwich

Vaughan, William, Esq.

* Walpole, Lord
* Warren, Peter, Esq. 2 Copies
* Warren, John Willing, Esq.
* Waters, Mrs. Bath

Wheelwright, Charles Apthorpe, Esq.

* Whitbread, Samuel, Esq. 5 Copies
* White, Mr. Bookseller, 9 Copies

Winder, Miss, Putney

Wood, George, Esq.

* Woodward, Mr. Bath

Woodward, Miss, Bath

* Wray, Mrs. Richmond, 2 Copies

Young, John, Esq.

ANECDOTES

OF

GEORGE FREDERICK HANDEL.

ANECDOTES

OF

GEORGE FREDERICK HANDEL.

I T has been a long received opinion, that the offspring of persons advanced in years are generally weak in frame as well as intellect, and evidently show the languor of the stock from which they sprung; but George Frederick Handel, the subject of the present Memoirs, is a strong instance that such conclusions are not founded in truth: for though his father at the time of his birth was sixty-one years of age, his son astonished the world as an uncommon example of early approach to excellence, great strength of constitution, and continued abilities.

/Handel was born on the 24th of February, 1686, at Hall, a city in the dutchy of Magdeburg, in the circle of Upper Saxony, where his father resided as a physician.) He was the child of a second marriage. His father destined him to the profession of the civil law; but Handel discovered in his early childhood a strong passion for music.

Few instances occur of a more early, decided, or fortunate propensity to a particular science. Pope said of himself that

" He lisp'd in numbers, and the numbers came;"

Handel, though he never possessed a fine voice, could sing as soon as he could speak, and evinced such a predilection for music, that the father carefully kept out of his reach all instruments, with the hopes of weaning his mind from what he deemed a degrading attachment. But the child contrived to obtain possession of a clavicord, which he secreted in the garret, and at night, when he was supposed to be asleep, the young enthusiast was awake; and the imagination may fondly view him striking the strings of his lyre,—that lyre which was to charm all Europe with its energy.

It is the property of Genius to possess that inflexible spirit, and unalterable adherence to a resolution once formed, which defies opposition, diminishes danger, and surmounts impediment: this disposition tyrannically checked, preys on the temper, and settles into gloominess and misanthropy; but if cherished, and warmed with moderate success, it produces the noblest and most expansive efforts of human energy. This disposition was the characteristic of Handel; and his inflexible spirit of perseverance is marked by a trivial occurrence, which took place in the seventh year of his age. His father, purposing to visit one of his sons, who was valet de chambre to the Duke of Saxe Weisenfeld, Handel earnestly intreated that he might be allowed to accompany him; but his request was peremptorily rejected. The father set off in a chaise; and when he had travelled a few miles, he was surprised at the sight of his son, who, with a strength greatly surpassing his years, had set out on foot and overtaken the carriage, the progress of which had been retarded by the badness of the roads. After a sharp animadversion, and some reluctance, the little suppliant was permitted to take his seat, and gratify his earnest desire of visiting his brother.

At the Duke's court, Handel was not so closely watched by his father, as at home. He enjoyed many opportunities of indulging his natural propensity; and he contrived, occasionally, to play upon the organ in the Duke's chapel at the conclusion of divine service. One morning the Duke hearing the organ touched in an unusual manner, inquired of his valet who was the performer. The valet replied that it was his brother; and mentioning at the same time his wonderful talents and predilection for music, and his father's repugnance, the Duke sent for them both. After other inquiries, the Duke was so much pleased with the spirit and talents of the boy, that he pleaded the cause of nature : he represented it as a crime against the public and posterity, to rob the world of such a genius; and, finally, persuaded the father to sacrifice his own scruples, and to permit his son to be instructed in the profession for which he had evinced so strong an inclination. A more interesting scene can hardly be conceived, than Handel listening to the arguments of his powerful advocate, and marking his final triumph over the reluctant prejudices of his parent. The Duke became so much interested in his success, that, at his departure, he made him a present, and promised his protection if he zealously applied to his studies.

At his return to Hall, his father placed him under the tuition of William Zackau, organist to the cathedral; a man of science and judgment. Zackau carefully instilled into his scholar, a thorough knowledge of the principles of harmony, and by explaining to him the different styles of Italian and German composition, he laid the foundation of that fame, which was to claim so distinguished a place in the annals of music. Handel made so rapid a progress, that before he had completed his seventh year, he was able to officiate on the organ for his master; and at the age of nine, he began to study composition. At this early period of his life he is said to have composed, every week, during three successive years, a spiritual cantata, or church service for voices, with instrumental accompaniments.*

Having exhausted his source of improvement at Hall, he became desirous of enlarging his knowledge, and was eager to obtain applause on a more distinguished theatre. He made choice of Berlin as the

* It has long been a matter of curious research among the admirers of Handel, to discover any traces of his early studies. Among Mr. Smith's collection of music, now in the possession of his daughter-in-law, Lady Rivers, is a book of manuscript music, dated 1698, and inscribed with the initials G. F. H. It was evidently a common-place book belonging to Handel in the fourteenth year of his age. The greater part is in his own hand, and the notes are characterized by a peculiar manner of forming the crotchets.

It contains various airs, choruses, capricios, fugues, and other pieces of music, with the names of contemporary musicians, such as Zackau, Alberti, Frobergher, Krieger, Kerl, Ebner, Strunch. They were probably exercises adopted at pleasure, or dictated for him to work upon, by his master. The composition is uncommonly scientific, and contains the seeds of many of his subsequent performances.

Sir John Hawkins says, that at the age of *nine*, Handel composed motetts for the service of the church, and continued to make one every week for three years. *Hist. of* spot, where the Opera, under the patronage of Frederick the First, was in a flourishing state, and boasted the aid of the most distinguished musicians of Italy; among whom Buononcini and Attilio were not the least conspicuous. The fame of Handel had preceded him; but these two musicians considered him a mere child, whose abilities had been greatly exaggerated: Buononcini, therefore, in order to try his skill, composed a cantata in the chromatic style, in which he comprized difficulties sufficient to puzzle an experienced master. Handel, however, treated this formidable composition as a mere trifle; he executed it at sight, with a degree of accuracy, truth, and expression, hardly to be expected from repeated practice, and from an aged performer.

But the display of congenial powers, did not impress Buononcini with one sentiment of friendship, or draw from him any symptom of kindness; though civil, he behaved to Handel with such reserve, as seemed to imply, that the foundation of future animosity was laid at that moment. Attilio, on the contrary, shewed him a partiality; the result of a generous and honourable disposition. He would place him for hours at his harpsichord, and was anxious to aid his progress in composition, or facilitate his readiness in execution.

Music. Dr. Burney observes, that when only ten years old, Handel composed a set of Sonatas in three parts. It seems as if they were published. He adds, that " Lord Marchmont picked them up in his travels, and that they are now in the King's Collection." The exercises to which Handel was accustomed, observes Sir John Hawkins, were compositions and fugues upon airs, or subjects delivered to him from time to time by his master. He adds, this is the mode of exercise for young proficients in music, and is also the test of a master.

Proud to patronize so promising a genius, Frederick frequently invited him to court, made him considerable presents, and, finally, proposed to send him to Italy at his own charge. This proposal Handel was eager to accept; but his father, foreseeing that it would impose a restraint on his son, declined; alleging as an excuse, that his very advanced age required his son's presence. In compliance with his father's injunctions Handel left Berlin, unwilling to expose himself to further solicitation.

Though Handel perfectly acquiesced in the propriety of the motives which induced his father to reject the proposal of Frederick, yet the flattering reception he had met with in his two excursions from home, opened to his view the fairest prospects of profit and celebrity. His father dying, a diminution in his mother's income induced him to repair to Hamburgh, where the Opera was next in repute to that of Berlin. On his arrival he secured an engagement at the opera-house, not as a principal performer on the harpsichord, but as second ripieno violin. So extraordinary a step of voluntary self-abasement will appear singular; but it was the effect of a principle unbecoming the dignity of a great mind, which led him to affect a simplicity, or rather humility of conduct, founded on vanity, and which his youth only could excuse, that he might enjoy the surprise excited by an unexpected display of his powers. Such an opportunity soon occurred. Reinhard Keiser, the leader of the band, encumbered with debts, was obliged to absent himself; and to the general astonishment, the unobserved performer on the violin took his seat before the harpsichord, and soon convinced his audience, and the band, that they had no reason to regret, but ought to exult in the change.

There is a received account of a contest for this enviable precedence, and an attempt to assassinate Handel, which was founded on a
misrepresentation of the following occurrence. Matheson, who was
afterwards Secretary to the English Resident, and wrote several books
on the subject of Music, was at that time a principal singer, and occasional composer. He had set to music the opera of Cleopatra, in
which he himself performed Antony; but his part being over in an
early period of the piece, it was his custom to take his seat at the
harpsichord, and conduct the band during the rest of the performance.
This had been submitted to by Keiser; but Handel was not of a
disposition so accommodating. He refused to resign his seat; and
Matheson, in a rage, as they were going down the steps of the orchestra at the close of the opera, gave him a blow. Their swords were
instantly drawn; but Matheson's weapon fortunately breaking against
his antagonist's button, put an end to the rencounter. They had been
in habits of intimacy, which they soon resumed; and were rejoiced at
the lucky conclusion of so serious an incident, arising from so trifling
a cause.

In addition to the profits of his engagement, Handel had scholars
sufficient to render all assistance from his mother unneccssary; and
he returned the first remittance she sent him, with a supply from his
savings. Before his quarrel with Matheson, he had travelled with him
to Lubeck, where there was a vacancy for the organist's place. They
performed this journey in the public caravan, with all the thoughtless
hilarity of youth, singing extempore duets, and amusing themselves
with all imaginable frolics on the road; to which the affected simplicity and archness of Handel gave an exquisite zest. Finding the

acceptance of the place coupled with a condition, that the organist was to take a wife, who was to be chosen for him by the magistrates, they each of them declined offering themselves on such conditions, and returned together to Hamburgh.

During his residence at Hamburgh, he composed his first Italian opera of Almira (1704). It met with great and flattering success, and ran thirty nights without intermission. The next year he produced Nerone; and the two succeeding years Florindo, and Dafne; all which were eminently successful. But he was at this time so much engaged with his scholars, and in the production of lessons for the harpsichord, that he did not give to the public so many operas as the fertility of his genius would have enabled him.

At this period the Prince of Tuscany, brother to the Grand Duke, came to Hamburgh, and engaged Handel's attention, by introducing to his notice a considerable variety of Italian music; dwelling with patriotic enthusiasm on the pre-eminence of his countrymen. He lamented that Handel had not visited a region, where every branch of the musical science was carried to the highest perfection, and offered his patronage if he would accompany him to Florence. Though Handel had been long desirous of going to Italy, he politely declined this offer, from a noble spirit of independence, which was never known to forsake him, even in the most distressful seasons of his life. But his visit was only postponed.

Having acquired a sufficient sum to defray his expences, he left Hamburgh in 1708, and repaired to Florence; where his reception was such as might be expected from the countenance of the exalted personage who introduced him. At Florence he composed the opera of Rodrigo, for which the Grand Duke presented him an hundred sequins, and a service of plate. From Florence he proceeded to Venice, where he arrived *incognito* at the Carnival, and was immediately discovered by Scarlatti, who, listening to him as he sat at the harpsichord in his visor, exclaimed, that the performer must be either the famous Saxon, or the devil.

(1709.) He was soon prevailed upon to compose the opera of Agrippina, and he effected it in three weeks, to the astonishment of Venice; and, as the author of so excellent and unexpected a performance, he was almost idolized. Agrippina was brought out at a theatre which had been shut up for a considerable time, but which was now crowded every night; and all the first singers from the other theatres offered to perform in the opera of *Il caro Sassone*. The audience knew no bounds in testifying their admiration. Vittoria, an excellent actress, singer, and favourite mistress of the Grand Duke of Tuscany, who had conceived an affection for Handel at Florence, came to Venice, and bore a principal part in the new opera. His youth and comeliness, joined to his musical fame, had made an impression on her heart; but Handel was too prudent to encourage an attachment, which might have occasioned the ruin of both.

From Venice he went to Rome, preceded by his illustrious reputation, which procured him the immediate patronage of Cardinal Ottoboni; for whom he composed several pieces in so masterly a style, as astonished, and even confounded the oldest proficients. He had trials of skill with eminent musicians, particularly with *Dominico Scarlatti*, who had the honour, in some measure, to divide the laurel with him; for though Handel was allowed a distinguished superiority on the organ, yet, on the harpsichord, the contest remained doubtful. Handel was also courted by Cardinals Pamfilio and Colonna. For Cardinal Pamfilio, who possessed the talent of making extempore poetry, Handel composed extempore music. Among these were *Il Trionfo del Tempo*, and a poem in praise of the Musician, wherein Pamfilio compared him to Orpheus.

From Rome he proceeded to Naples, where he was no less the object of esteem and admiration; and at the request of Donna Laura, a Spanish princess, he composed *Acige e Galatea*.* He then made a second visit to Florence, Rome, and Venice, and at length resolved to quit Italy, where his reputation had acquired a lustre exceeding his most sanguine expectations. He was distinguished, according to the custom of the country, by the appellation of *Il Sassone;* and had he remained in Italy, that distinction would have superseded his patronimic. Though his productions at the time were numerous, few are now extant, except the pieces which have been alluded to.

After his return to Germany, (1710) he visited Hanover. Steffani, a learned and elegant composer, whom he had known at Venice, and who was a great favourite at the Electoral court, introduced him to the notice of the Princess Sophia, and her grandson the Electoral

* This was totally different from the serenata written by Gay, and so well known in England. The Italian names of Handel's operas are generally preserved in his Life, to distinguish them from his English compositions.

Prince, afterwards George the Second.   Baron Kilmanseg, who had
been acquainted with him in Italy, recommended him to the attention
of the Elector, afterwards George the First; who, struck with his merit,
proposed to retain him in his service, with a salary of fifteen hundred
crowns per annum.   This liberal offer Handel accepted; but on condition, that he should be permitted to visit England, whither he had
been invited by many persons of high rank, whom he had seen in Italy,
and at Hanover.   The Elector agreed to these conditions; and afterwards, by the friendly interference of Steffani, appointed him master
of the chapel.   In his way to England he visited his native city, where
he paid his duty to his mother, who was blind and infirm, and renewed
his intimacy with his relations and friends, amongst whom Zackau was
not forgotten.   At Dusseldorf he had a flattering reception from the
Elector Palatine, who presented him with a service of plate, and wished
to retain him in his Court.

In England, (1710) observes Dr. Burney, his reception was as flattering to himself, as honourable to the nation; at this time no less
successful in war than in the cultivation of the arts of peace.   To the
wit, poetry, literature, and science, which marked this period of our
history, Handel added all the blandishments of a nervous and learned
music, which he first brought hither, planted, and lived to see grow to
a very flourishing state.   The impatience of the public was so great,
that Handel was immediately employed in setting to music the opera
of Rinaldo, which was prepared and finished with unparalleled haste.
Aaron Hill, who was manager of the opera, sketched the plan from
Tasso's *Gierusalemme Liberata,* and Rossi, the Italian poet, composed
the drama.   In his Preface, Rossi commends Handel's musical talents

in the highest strain of panegyric, and calls him the Orpheus of the
age. He observes, that Handel scarcely allowed him time to write the
words; and that, to his great astonishment, he set the whole to music
in the short space of a fortnight. The principal part was written for
Nicolini, whose graceful and expressive action was praised by Steele,
in the Tatler.* Rinaldo was received with the greatest applause, not
only on its first appearance, but on three subsequent revivals; and
Walsh, the music seller, is reputed to have gained fifteen hundred
pounds by printing the scores.

Having staid in England near a twelvemonth, during which his
execution was no less admired than his compositions, Handel took
leave of Queen Anne, who accompanied several valuable presents
with expressions of regret at his departure, and wishes for his speedy
return; which he respectfully promised should take place as soon as
he could obtain permission of the Elector.

On his arrival at Hanover, Handel composed twelve chamber duets,
and a few other pieces of little importance; and soon obtained permission to return to England, on the positive assurance that he would
not long absent himself from the Electoral dominions. His return to
London was hailed by the musical world as a national acquisition, and
every measure was adopted to render his abode pleasant and perma-
nent. An eminent occasion was not long wanting for the full exercise
of his great talents. He was called upon to compose the Grand
Jubilate, and Te Deum, for the conclusion of the peace of Utrecht.
In that composition he acquitted himself with all that wonderful effect

* No. 115.

of sublimity and judgment, for which he was remarkable. He also composed for the Opera-house, Teseo, and Il Pastor Fido; and both operas were well received. The Queen was so captivated with his performances, that she settled on him an annual pension of two hundred pounds, and the nobility vied with each other in proving their esteem for so distinguished a musician; who, thus rewarded, courted, and patronized, forgot his promise of returning to Germany.

In 1714 Queen Anne died. The accession of his liberal patron, who, under the title of George the First, succeeded to the throne, under other circumstances would have been the moment of exultation; but instead of appearing in the foremost rank of congratulators, Handel did not venture to present himself at Court. From this embarrassment, however, he was happily relieved by the kindness of Baron Kilmanseg, Master of the Horse to George the First as Elector of Hanover. Apprized that his Majesty had projected a party on the Thames, he informed Handel of the King's intention: Handel immediately produced that celebrated composition, known by the title of the Water Music. Having procured a band, he followed the barge, and watching his opportunity, unexpectedly charmed the Royal party by melodies of singular effect and sweetness. The King inquiring who was the composer of that exquisite harmony, Baron Kilmanseg said that it was Handel; stated his contrition, and sued for his restoration to favour. This respectful attempt at reconciliation, and atonement for his conduct, mollified the Sovereign. Soon afterwards, Geminiani was commanded to play, in the King's closet, twelve solos which he had recently composed: fearful that their proper effect would be lost by an indifferent accompaniment, he expressed a wish that Handel might be permitted to preside at the harpsichord. This request was conveyed to the King, and enforced by the friendly solicitation of the Baron. Handel was restored to favour; and the King increased the pension granted by Queen Anne to four hundred pounds a year.

In the course of the summer, Handel passed several months at Barn Elms, in Surrey, with Mr. Andrews; and in the winter, at that gentleman's house in town. He was also invited (1715) to the mansion of the Earl of Burlington, where he composed Amadige, or Amadis de Gaul; the only opera of his which appeared (May 15,) on the boards of the King's Theatre for five years. He remained three years with Lord Burlington, during which time he became acquainted with Pope, Gay, and Arbuthnot. Pope not only had no knowledge of the science of music, but received no gratification from " the concord of sweet sounds." He heard the performances of Handel with perfect indifference, if not impatience. Gay was pleased with music without understanding it, but forgot the performance when the notes ceased to vibrate. Arbuthnot, on the contrary, who was a judge of music, and a composer, felt the merits of Handel, and conceived an esteem for him, which he afterwards displayed under the most trying circumstances. From the Earl of Burlington's, Handel went to Cannons, the seat of the Duke of Chandos, where he remained two years as composer for the chapel; producing numerous anthems and other sacred pieces, and the English serenata of Acis and Galatea.

During the last year (1720) of his residence at Cannons, the principal nobility and gentry resolved to establish an Academy of Music. The King was the patron, and subscribed one thousand pounds; and the whole subscription amounted to fifty thousand pounds. Application being made to Handel to assume the management, he consented; and, having set off for Dresden to procure singers, returned with Senesino, and several other performers, prepared to open the Opera-house in a style of superior splendour. He first produced for the Academy the Opera of Radamisto; the great success of which evinced his talents as a composer, and a happy power of adapting airs to the abilities of the respective singers. Radamisto proved as great a favourite in London, as Agrippina had proved at Venice; and disappointed crowds went every night from the house, unable to obtain seats. The great success of Handel did not, however, exempt him from the rivalship of Buononcini and Attilio. They had been invited to England by the former managers of the Opera; and as they were composers of acknowledged merit, their admirers refused to concede the precedence to Handel. Hence arose those musical feuds, which Swift has ridiculed as a dispute,

"'Twixt Tweedle-dum, and Tweedle-dee,"

and which were brought to a crisis in the succeeding winter. It was agreed by the friends of the three rivals, that each of them should compose an act of the Opera of Mutius Scævola, and an overture. Buononcini set the first act, Attilio the second, and Handel the third. The preference was given to Handel; he was appointed composer; the Academy was finally established, and the Opera prosperously conducted during nine years.

During this period he composed fifteen Operas, all of which possessed extraordinary merit, and were highly successful; but either from mismanagement in the pecuniary concerns of the house, or from the impossibility of supporting an Opera in London, without constant contributions, the condition of the treasury became so unprosperous, that the whole sum subscribed, was in this short and brilliant period entirely exhausted, and the Academy dissolved. This is the real cause of the termination of this splendid undertaking, though it has been ignorantly ascribed to the irritability of Handel. It is true, indeed, that the composer was not of a temper to treat singers with great respect ; he considered them, perhaps too much, as mere instruments, which gave utterance to that harmony, of which he was so distinguished an Author. He possessed the impetuosity and inflexibility of genius. On the contrary, Senesino, intoxicated with popular applause, which his talents well merited, did not bend with implicit submission to the wishes of the manager. Disputes certainly ran high between Handel and Senesino, before the dissolution of the Academy; but it is not true, that their irreconcilable antipathy was the occasion of that event. Senesino sung in operas composed by Handel, and under his management, two years after the dissolution had taken place.

If Handel was little disposed to submit to the caprice of the male performèrs, he was not of a temper patiently to endure the disturbance arising from female squabbles for precedence; and still less, to have his views thwarted by their peevishness, or non-compliance with rules which he had thought necessary to prescribe. His choler on such occasions surmounted all bounds of discretion. When Cuzzoni had refused to sing an air which he had composed for her, he exclaimed in a rage, that he well knew that she had the spirit of a devil; but that he would convince her whom she had to deal with, in dealing with him, for that he was Beelzebub, the Prince of the Devils; and seizing her by the waist, threatened to throw her from the window, if she persisted in her refusal. The pride and haughtiness of Cuzzoni, and Faustina, was of that description, that neither of them would sing when the other was present; and persons of the first distinction humoured this insolence, by enlisting in parties, and degrading themselves by the most unworthy condescensions. But their quarrels with Handel had little effect to the prejudice of the Academy, for Cuzzoni sung for him at the same time with Senesino.

At the close of the last season (1728) of the Academy, the singers dispersed, and during a whole year there was no Italian Opera in London. In this interval, Handel being determined, in conjunction with Heidegger, to establish Operas on their private account, went to Italy in search of performers. He returned (1729) with a respectable band, and opened the house (29th December) with Lotario; which, together with Parthenope, were sufficient attractions for the season. The following year, Senesino sung for him in various Operas, and continued to perform till Handel's dissensions with him and Cuzzoni became so violent, that they could no longer remain united.

An opposition was immediately excited by many persons of distinction, who had taken umbrage that they were excluded from their subscription boxes; and that the price of admission was raised to a guinea when Oratorios were performed. These imprudent measures gave birth to a rival Opera, at the theatre in Lincoln's Inn Fields; which was patronized by many persons of quality, and to which several of the singers and instrumental performers, whom Handel had engaged, deserted.   Senesino complained that Handel no longer composed for him in his usual style; he therefore quitted his theatre, and Cuzzoni accompanied him.

Handel, however, was not to be intimidated. Carestini, Strada, the Negri family, Durastanti, and Scalzi, still remained; and he possessed that powerful resource which never failed him, his own immeasurable abilities. It is not intended to describe the progress of this contest, which ruined Handel's finances, impaired his health, and even affected his understanding. He fought manfully, changed alternately to the Haymarket, Lincoln's Inn Fields, and Covent Garden Theatre, varying his performers, and even his style of music. Yet such was the inveteracy of the opposing party, that though his Operas were most admirable compositions, and those of his adversaries far inferior in merit, the tide of fashion set decidedly against him.

In this arduous situation, which lasted near eleven years, he displayed great superiority and force of mind. He did not condescend to conciliate favour by degrading concession, or to reduce the expence, by engaging inferior performers, or diminishing the salaries of those whom he employed. On the contrary, his band was always numerous, well selected, and liberally paid; but so long a contest, with such expensive exertions, and such unfavourable consequences, could not fail alike to injure the body and the mind. Handel evinced, in the course of the struggle, occasional symptoms of mental derangement, and lost the use of his right arm by a stroke of the palsy. Suffering under this affliction, he went immediately to Tunbridge, and from thence to Aix-la-Chapelle.

In the days of his prosperity he had invested a considerable sum in the funds; but at the end of this pertinacious opposition he had lost ten thousand pounds, the produce of his youthful exertions, and was besides so greatly in debt, that he was in daily fear of being arrested for the salaries of his performers; with whom, however, he contrived to settle by bonds, which were afterwards duly discharged. It is not the least astonishing part of his character, that his promptitude of invention, and brilliancy of ideas, in all this time did not forsake him. At the moment of his recovery (1737) from a violent illness, and even attended with fits of lunacy, his faculties were exerted with their full vigour in bringing forward the Opera of Faramond; and in composing the funeral anthem on the death of his lamented patroness, Queen Caroline, equal in pathos and sublimity to his best compositions.

Nor had his enemies any cause to exult. Though Handel gave up the contest, no victory was gained by them; though he was impoverished, they were not enriched. It is clearly ascertained, that without considerable subscriptions, great abilities in the composers, excellence in the singers, and strenuous exertions, an Opera can never be advantageously maintained in London. When all the patronage and the best singers were enlisted on one side, and the best composers on the other, it was easy to suppose that both undertakings would fail. The public always sided with Handel; but the public, except of the higher class of society, are not sufficiently attached to the Italian Opera, to give celebrity and profit to the undertaking. To be sensible of the beauties of Italian music, requires an intimacy with the science, and a knowledge of the language. Few possess those advantages. The language of Nature is open to all, whether in expression or action; but the grace of expression and action is not sufficient to engage the attention of mankind, where sense is concealed by an unknown idiom, and the understanding is not gratified by a perception of appropriate harmony.

Handel could not complain of neglect. Though Farinelli and the nobility at that time opposed him; though he had no capital singer except Strada, and laboured under other disadvantages, his Alexander's Feast (19th February, 1736) was attended by an audience uncommonly numerous. Thirteen hundred persons were assembled at the Theatre of Covent Garden, and the receipt of the house amounted to four hundred and fifty pounds. His benefit at the Haymarket, in the following month (28th March, 1738), was equally well attended; the pit was laid into boxes, and the house crowded in every part. He received an honourable mark of distinction from the liberality of an individual, seldom conferred on any man during his life. His statue, admirably sculptured by Roubillac, was placed by Mr. Jonathan Tyers in the gardens at Vauxhall (1738); and the public coincided in the justice and propriety of the compliment paid to his merit.

It may be alleged, in contradiction to Handel's popularity, that several of his Operas, published in this interval by subscription, barely defrayed the expences; but it is to be observed, that the most important and beneficial class of subscribers, were adverse to his interests; and that the number of rival composers who advanced their claims to the patronage of the public, though they could not contest the palm, interfered and lessened his profits.

At length (1741) Handel determined to abandon Opera compositions. He had already produced thirty-nine Operas for the English stage; all excellent, and possessing that infinite variety, which his musical talents were capable of producing. His last Opera was Deidamia; which, though abounding in beauties, was received with indifference, and performed but three nights. The flattering reception which Handel had met with when he visited Oxford, where he was offered the degree of Doctor in Music, but declined accepting it, induced him to try the event of a journey to Ireland. He was received at Dublin with such strong marks of approbation, as did no less honour to him, than to the taste of the nation. His Messiah, which was reported to have been coldly received in London, * was applauded with all the enthusiasm due to claims of such uncommon excellence. He remained in Ireland about nine months, and acquired every advantage which health, fame, and profit, could bestow. The public in his absence had become fully sensible of his merits; Arbuthnot had ever been his friend, and written pamphlets in his favour, while the opposition against him was in its full force; Pope, more economical of praise, now ventured that compliment in the Dunciad, which acknowledges his title to musical fame; and Handel no longer had to contend with prejudices, or combat the malignancy of inveterate opposition.

As from this period Handel must be considered as the composer of Oratorios, it will be proper to give a short account of their rise and progress. His first Oratorio was Esther; which was composed

* Dr. Burney has been at the laudable pains to disprove the fact, and has succeeded in rendering it doubtful.

in 1720, for the Duke of Chandos, at Cannons; but was not given to the public till eleven years after, when it was performed by the children of the King's chapel. The chorus was sung after the manner of the ancients, and the singers were placed between the stage and the orchestra. The instrumental performers were, principally, gentlemen belonging to the Philharmonic Society. This novel species of entertainment was so greatly approved, that the representation was repeated at the Crown and Anchor. Their success inspired Handel with new hopes. Esther was again performed at the Haymarket, in 1733: it ran ten nights; and with the addition of Handel's concertos on the organ, then new to the public, proved sufficiently attractive. He next produced Deborah: and in his journey to Oxford in the same year, Athalia. In the succeeding year he revived Acis and Galatea, set to music Alexander's Feast, Israel in Egypt, L'Allegro ed il Penseroso, Saul, and the Messiah.

After his return from Ireland, he continued every year the same style of composition, and generally with the greatest success; though with occasional failures, owing to the latent seeds of former animosity. His merit and perseverance were amply rewarded; he retained a firm hold of the public favour and patronage to the end of his life; and he was not only enabled to clear himself from all incumbrances, but to realize a fortune of twenty thousand pounds.

Some years before his death (1751), he was afflicted with a gutta serena, which, as he justly apprehended, in the end deprived him of sight; though he underwent the operation of couching. His spirits for a short time sunk under this affliction; but when he found the evil incurable, he submitted with resignation. Unable without as-sistance to conduct the Oratorios, he applied to his pupil and long-tried friend Mr. Smith, and by his assistance they were continued.

It was a most affecting spectacle to see the venerable musician, whose efforts had charmed the ear of a discerning public, led by the hand of friendship to the front of the stage, to make an obeisance of acknowledgment to his enraptured audience.

When Handel became blind, though he no longer presided over the Oratorios, he still introduced concertos on the organ between the acts. At first he relied on his memory, but the exertion becoming painful to him, he had recourse to the inexhaustible stores of his rich and fertile imagination. He gave to the band, only such parts of his intended composition, as were to be filled up by their accompaniment; and relied on his own powers of invention to produce, at the impulse of the moment, those captivating passages, which arrested attention, and enchanted his auditors.

It is curious, though painful to a thinking mind, to trace the com-parison between Homer, Milton, and Handel; all of them deprived of sight, and each exerting his faculties under that severe visitation, to the wonder of an admiring world. The singular and sublime talents of Milton, displayed in his Paradise Lost, were better known indeed to posterity, than to his contemporaries. The merits of that animated composition, were gradually unfolded; but the Grecian Bard sang his Iliad and Odyssey amidst the praises of his admiring countrymen. Handel though a foreigner, yet with talents equally sublime, and

E

melody not inferior, heard his own fame resounded in the loud tribute
of deserved commendation.

Nature at last became exhausted, he exhibited evident symptoms
of decay; his appetite failed him, and he saw without dismay his dissolution approaching. But his extraordinary faculties continued to the
end of his life: his last public performance (6th April, 1759) took
place only a week before he died (14th April); and that great event
happened, as he had often expressed his earnest wish, on Good Fri-
day. He was buried in Westminster Abbey; his funeral sermon was
preached by Dr. Pearce, Bishop of Rochester; and at his own expence a marble monument was erected to his memory, by the sculpture
of Roubillac. His figure is represented standing before the organ, and
listening to the harp of an Angel. On a scroll are recorded his own
divine notes, set to those emphatical words, comprising the sum of
Christian hope, " I know that my Redeemer liveth."

George Frederick Handel, was seventy-three years of age when he
died. He was large in person, and his natural corpulency, which increased as he advanced in life, rendered his whole appearance of that
bulky proportion, as to give rise to Quin's inelegant, but forcible
expression; that his hands were feet, and his fingers toes. From a
sedentary life, he had contracted a stiffness in his joints, which in
addition to his great weight and weakness of body, rendered his gait
awkward; still his countenance was open, manly, and animated;
expressive of all that grandeur and benevolence, which were the
prominent features of his character. In temper he was irascible,
impatient of contradiction, but not vindictive; jealous of his musical

pre-eminence, and tenacious in all points, which regarded his professional honour.

He was averse to all restraint on his freedom. Being informed at
the Spa, that the King of Prussia was expected, and purposed to be
witness of his musical powers, to the great disappointment of the
monarch, he quitted the place some days before his arrival; unwilling to expose himself to solicitations he had determined not to
comply with, or to commands which he could not resist. In England
he was always well received and warmly patronized; but his general
aversion to subscription engagements, and the resolute inflexibility of
his temper, prevented the accession of some friends, and alienated
others. With conscious pride, he was unwilling to be indebted but to
his own abilities for his advancement, and they finally triumphed over
all his opposers.

His chief foible was a culpable indulgence in the sensual gratifications of the table; but this foible was amply compensated by a
sedulous attention to every religious duty, and moral obligation. His
understanding was excellent, and his knowledge extensive. Besides
the German, his native tongue, he was intimate with the English, and
master of the Latin, French, and Italian languages : he had acquired
a taste for painting, which he improved during his residence in Italy,
and felt great pleasure in contemplating the works of art. His great
delight was derived from his attachment to his own science, and he
experienced particular satisfaction from religious principles, in presiding
at the organ in the cathedral church of St. Paul. He frequently declared in conversation, the high gratification he enjoyed in setting the

Scriptures to music, and how greatly he was edified by contemplating the sublime passages abounding in the sacred writings.

From the same motive he was regular in his attendance on divine service, at his parish church near Hanover Square, where his devout posture of humility, and earnestness of voice and gesture, avowing his faith, acknowledging his errors, and appealing to his Maker for mercy, were strongly impressive.

Handel contracted few intimacies, and when his early friends died, he was not solicitous of acquiring new ones. He was never married; but his celibacy must not be attributed to any deficiency of personal attractions, or to the source which Sir John Hawkins unjustly supposes, the want of social affection. On the contrary, it was owing to the independency of his disposition, which feared degradation, and dreaded confinement. For when he was young, two of his scholars, ladies of considerable fortune, were so much enamoured of him, that each was desirous of a matrimonial alliance. The first is said to have fallen a victim to her attachment. Handel would have married her; but his pride was stung by the coarse declaration of her mother, that she never would consent to the marriage of her daughter with a fiddler; and, indignant at the expression, he declined all further intercourse. After the death of the mother, the father renewed the acquaintance, and informed him that all obstacles were removed; but he replied, that the time was now past; and the young lady fell into a decline, which soon terminated her existence. The second attachment, was a lady splendidly related, whose hand he might have obtained by renouncing his profession. That condition he resolutely refused, and laudably declined the connection which was to prove a restriction on the great faculties of his mind.

Handel's religious disposition was not a mere display, it was amply productive of religion's best fruit, charity; and this liberal sentiment not only influenced him in the day of prosperity, but even when standing on the very brink of ruin. He performed Acis and Galatea (1740), for the benefit of the musical fund: the next year he gave them his Epithalamium, called *Parnasso in Festa*, and further extended his kindness by a legacy of one thousand pounds. He was no less bountiful to the Foundling Hospital; his early exertions in its favour were the principal support of that respectable establishment. He gave an organ to the chapel; and an annual benefit, by which seven thousand pounds was cleared in the course of a few years. He also presented the governors with the original score of the Messiah. His charity was by no means restricted to public donations, he was equally attentive to the claims of friendship, affection, and gratitude. The widow of his master Zackau, being old and poor, received from him frequent remittances; and her son would have enjoyed the benefits of his liberality; but for his profligacy, and incurable drunkenness. The bulk of Handel's fortune was bequeathed to his relations. All his music he left to Mr. Smith.

There is not any circumstance more delightful to the eye of contemplation, than to observe great talents exerted in the cause of benevolence and humanity. Mason has most beautifully described its effects upon the mind.—

" Humanity, thy awful strain shall greet the ear
     " Sonorous, sweet, and clear.
" And as amidst the dulcet notes that breathe
        " From flute or lyre,
" The deep base rolls its manly melody,
        " Guiding the tuneful choir:
      " So thou, Humanity, shalt lead along
      " The accordant passions in this moral song,
" And give one mental concert, truest harmony."

To the literary world he owed little obligation. Arbuthnot, indeed,
was his friend. Pope, notwithstanding his high compliment, slighted,
and Swift ridiculed him: but that patronage, which had first reflected
favour, and conferred honour on him, was the countenance shewn to
him by the illustrious house of Brunswick. George the First had
settled on him a pension of £200. a year, in addition to that already
granted by Anne; George the Second added a pension of equal
amount, in reward for teaching the Royal Children; these munificent
donations formed his support in the hour of his adversity, and the
habit of confining his expences adhered to him through life. He
frequently presided at those concerts which were held in the royal
library, and was remarkable for enforcing decorum and attention;
though the performers, and the audience, were persons of the first
distinction. The King, and Prince and Princess of Wales, were ever
fond of his music, and attended his Oratorios, even when they were
so much deserted, that Lord Chesterfield wittily, but ill naturedly
called attending an oratorio, " an intrusion on his Majesty's pri-
vacy."

His own death deprived him of the patronage which would have resulted from the acknowledged taste of the present Sovereign. But it ought not, in the life of Handel, to be omitted, that, though that gratification was denied, the British Monarch presided at the Commemoration of Handel; the most splendid tribute ever paid to posthumous fame.

In the same Abbey where his body lies interred, those anthems which he had composed for the funeral service of Queen Caroline, together with the most celebrated pieces of his compositions, were judiciously selected for the celebration of his own memory; and performed in the highest style of instrumental perfection and vocal excellence. It was an honour to the profession, to the nation, and to the Sovereign.

The genius and abilities of Handel, were truly gigantic, and Pope justly said of him,

> " Strong in new arms the giant Handel stands,
> " Like bold Briareus with a hundred hands."

No species of composition escaped him; the wonderful force of his execution was as astonishing as the vast efforts of his mind. He made the organ his own instrument; and Scarlatti declared, that, till he heard Handel, he had no conception of his powers. Akenside, in delineating the character of Shakspeare remarks, that

> " Different minds
> " Incline to different objects :—one pursues

" The vast alone, the wonderful, the wild :

" Another sighs for harmony and grace,

" And gentlest beauty.   Hence, when lightning flies

" The arch of heaven, and thunders rock the ground;

" When furious whirlwinds rend the howling air,

" And ocean groaning from the lowest bed,

" Heaves his tempestuous billows to the sky,

" Amid the mighty uproar, while below,

" The nations tremble, Shakspeare looks abroad

" From some high cliff superior, and enjoys

" The elemental war."——   *Pleasures of Imag.*   Book iii.

The distinction due to Shakspeare in energy of poetry, to Michael Angelo in sculpture and painting, Handel may justly claim in the sister art; to him belongs the Majesty of Music. The merit of Handel is not confined: it is of that universal cast, that he may be styled the great musician of nature. Though he was not able to pronounce the English with correctness, he thoroughly comprehended its nature and effects. In the funeral anthems, and the oratorios selected from the Scriptures, the words were principally chosen by himself; and the devotion of sounds, if the expression may be allowed, is in unison with the dignity, simple piety, and grandeur of the sacred writings. An English audience should estimate his abilities, by English compositions; and in beauty of expression and strong sense, he had there the greatest advantage: for what drama can be compared among all his Italian music, to the Acis and Galatea of Gay, L'Allegro and Penseroso of Milton, Dryden's unrivalled Ode to St. Cecilia, and Handel's great master-piece, the Messiah?

Words are, in relation to music, too frequently neglected, and considered as the mere vehicle for sounds; but sounds should be analogous to thoughts.

" To make the soul mount on a jig to heaven,"

is as absurd as to compose anthem music to ludicrous language. When sound and sense are judiciously united, in a fortunate illustration of each other; then articulation, the first principle in music, like light thrown upon a picture, discovers all the beauty of the subject, as well as merit of the execution.

The prejudice of fashion, and paucity of soprano voices in our own country, has too often occasioned an inadequate performance of Handel's music. Miss Linley proved to Handel, what Garrick was to Shakspeare; and those who recollect her captivating voice, feel the full merit of the great master's mind. A new light was thrown upon his compositions, and those who attended the Commemoration in Westminster Abbey, that spring-tide of harmony, have heard him in all his glory.

To specify Handel's claims to professional pre-eminence, would be a voluminous task; it would be no less than to select a variety of passages from each of his works, vocal as well as instrumental. Few men composed more; no man better. Handel was in music all things to all persons; considered generally he was irresistible, and master of the passions; the audience feel it, and in the language of that poetry, which he himself so happily made the strong example of his art,

" The list'ning crowd admire the lofty sound."

F

Such is the force and effect of his productions;—but he has the highest claim for moral and religious excellence. His pen was never debased to the disgraceful practice of an effeminate or seductive style of composition: it is entitled to the first attribute of praise.—It is sublime, affecting, animated, and devoted, without the gloom of superstition, to the service of God.

ANECDOTES

OF

JOHN CHRISTOPHER SMITH.

JOHN CHRISTOPHER SMITH.

From an Original Picture Painted by Zoffani

Published May 1.1799. by Cadell & Davies Strand

ANECDOTES

OF

JOHN CHRISTOPHER SMITH.

———————————————————

JOHN CHRISTOPHER SMITH was born in 1712. His father John Christopher Schmidt, * of Anspach in Franconia, after receiving a good education in the university of Halle, married a lady with a portion of seven thousand crowns, and settled in his native city. He carried on a considerable branch of traffic in the woollen trade, in which he might have acquired a large fortune, had he not been seduced by his passion for music; when Handel arrived at Anspach in 1716, he renewed an acquaintance which had commenced at Halle, and soon became so captivated with that great master's powers, that he left his wife and children in Germany, and accompanied Handel to England, where he regulated the expences of his public performance, and filled the office of treasurer with great exactness and fidelity. On the fourth year of his residence in England, he sent for his wife and family, which consisted of a son and two daughters

* Schmidt was the German name corresponding with the English appellation Smith.

Soon after his arrival, his son, the subject of these Anecdotes, was sent to Clare's Academy, in Soho Square. During this early period of his life, he too imbibed a fondness for music, and gave signs of a strong propensity to that science; and as his passion increased with his years, Handel offered to become his master. Accordingly, in the thirteenth year of his age, he was taken from the Academy, and placed under the tuition of Handel.

When Smith was about fourteen, chance threw him in the way of Dr. Samuel Clarke, author of the Sermons on the Attributes of God, and of other celebrated writings, who behaved to him with the kindness of a father. He one day said to him, " you follow a dangerous profession, which may lead you into late hours, and excesses of all kinds, that will injure your constitution, and corrupt your morals. Come to my house whenever you are at leisure, and play with my boy." Dr. Clarke's son was then about twelve years of age. Young Smith accepted this invitation with gratitude, and passed many happy hours at the Doctor's; who was often one of the party, and would ride upon a broomstick with him and his son.

That good man and excellent divine, not unfrequently instructed him in the rudiments of natural and revealed religion, in a manner adapted to his capacity. In his advanced age, Mr. Smith often dwelt on the recollection of Dr. Clarke's extreme condescension and good nature. He seldom mentioned, without strong emotions of gratitude, the great advantage which he derived from his exhortations and instructions, and was often heard to declare, that to him, under Providence, he was principally indebted for those principles of morality, and firm belief in Revelation, which never forsook him.

Under the tuition of Handel Smith made so considerable a proficiency in music, that in the eighteenth year of his age, he commenced teacher, and instantly obtained, through his master's recommendation, and his own merit, so much employment, as to enable him to maintain himself without assistance from his father.

He often mentioned with conscious pride, that he was never in debt but once, when he borrowed ten guineas of old Schudi, and that he was not easy till he had returned the sum. His prudence, however, never degenerated into narrow parsimony. He once met with a family in the greatest distress, and though he was at that time worth but one guinea, he gave half to them. A gentleman, whose daughter he taught, being informed of this humane action, gave him five guineas, as a mark of approbation. In this present, the poor family participated.

It was Smith's good fortune to become acquainted with Dr. Arbuthnot, who behaved to him with the affection of a father, and contributed, by his skill and advice, to the preservation of his life. At the age of eighteen he had so greatly injured his health, by intense application, that he was declared by Dr. Mead to be in a decline. Arbuthnot was of opinion, that relaxation and change of air might possibly restore him; and having an house at Highgate, invited him to pass the summer in that healthy situation. The Doctor told him that he would certainly fall a victim to his application, if he did not relax; and though he lent him an horse, would not suffer him to ride to

London, lest he might be tempted to resume his studies. By this kind care, his health was so far re-established, that he was again enabled to follow his profession. Thus the Doctor verified Pope's eulogium.

" He knows his art, but not his trade."

At Dr. Arbuthnot's house he frequently met Swift, Pope, Gay, and Congreve; a society highly improving to a young man. He observed that they never seemed desirous of uttering wise sayings, or witty repartees, but the conversation usually turned upon interesting subjects, when their talents and knowledge were displayed without ostentation. Sensible that Pope had no taste for music, he took an opportunity of inquiring what motive could induce him to celebrate Handel's praise so highly in his Dunciad. Pope replied, that merit, in every branch or science, ought to be encouraged; that the extreme illiberality with which many persons had joined to ruin Handel, in opposing his Operas, called forth his indignation; and though nature had denied his being gratified by Handel's uncommon talents in the musical line, yet when his powers were generally acknowledged, he thought it incumbent upon him to pay a tribute due to genius.

Although Handel had instructed his pupil in the rudiments of music, yet he could not stoop to the drudgery of teaching composition; and the scholar finding that he had not acquired sufficient knowledge, applied to Dr. Pepusch* and Rosengrave,† from both of whom, in

---

* John Christopher Pepusch, called by Sir John Hawkins one of the greatest theoretic musicians of the modern times, was born at Berlin in 1667, and acquired such an early reputation for his skill and execution, that he was appointed, at the age of fourteen,

particular from Roseingrave, he derived great advantage. With a view to profit by Roseingrave's kindness, he took lodgings in the same

to teach the Electoral Prince, afterwards Frederick William, the harpsichord. About the twentieth year of his age he went to Holland, and came to England after the Revolution, where he settled. Having attracted notice by various musical publications, he obtained the degree of Doctor of Music in the university of Oxford. He was employed by the Duke of Chandos, as his master of the chapel at Cannons, and composed many anthems, together with the morning and evening services. He set to music several masques and pieces for the Theatre; and assisted Gay in selecting tho tunes for the Beggar's Opera. Having married Margaretta de l'Epine, a celebrated singer, who quitted the stage with a fortune of ten thousand pounds, he not long afterwards relinquished composition; applied himself chiefly to the theory of music; and was fond of explaining the mysteries of the science to young professors, which induced Mr. Smith to court his assistance.

In 1717, he was appointed organist of the Charter House, which afforded him an adequate retreat, well suited to his time of life, and love of study. Here he was visited and consulted as an oracle; not only by young musical students, to whom he was always kind and communicative, but even by masters.

At the latter period of his life, he devoted himself to the study of Grecian music, and endeavoured to illustrate the doctrine of Isaac Vossius, concerning the rythm of the ancients. He was elected a Fellow of the Royal Society in 1746, and died in 1752, aged eighty-five. He was buried in the chapel of the Charter House; and several members of the Academy of Ancient Music, of which he was one of the original founders, and principal supporters, gratefully erected a monument to his memory.

If it be true what is said of him, that he treated all music, in which there was any fancy or invention, with sovereign contempt, and that he did not acquiesce in Handel's superior merit, calling him a good practical musician; his kindness in instructing Smith, who was the scholar and adorer of Handel, in the theory of music, reflects great honour on his candour and liberality of sentiment.

† Thomas Roseingrave, the son of Daniel Roseingrave, first organist of the Cathedral

house, in Wigmore-street, Mary-le-Bone, and received great advantage from his instruction. During this time, Roseingrave was a constant guest at his table, which was the only recompence he would ever receive. Smith always mentioned his name in terms of gratitude, and related anecdotes of his kind and friendly instructor.

of Salisbury, and in 1698 of St. Patrick's, Dublin. He received a classical education, which he completed at the Irish university, and was intended for one of the learned professions ; but though he was a very good scholar, his love for music led him to apply with so much zeal to that study, that his father, foreseeing that it would impede his success in any other line, permitted him to follow the bent of his genius, and sent him to Italy, where he became the friend of Scarlatti. On quitting Italy, he settled in London, and obtained the place of organist to St. George's church, Hanover Square. There were three candidates, Roseingrave, Stanley, who was then a very young man, and Topham, who, besides his knowledge in music, was an adept in the pugilistic art. Roseingrave played first upon the organ, and his performance charmed and astonished every person present, and no one more than Topham ; who observed, he could never stand in competition with him for music, but humorously added, that he would box with him whenever he pleased. Roseingrave was elected.

His reputation was at this period so high, that on commencing teacher, he might have gained one thousand pounds a year ; but an unfortunate event reduced him to extreme distress.

Among Roseingrave's scholars, was a young lady to whom he was greatly attached, and whose affections he had gained ; but her father, who intended to give her a large fortune, did not approve of her marrying a musician, and forbade Roseingrave his house. This disappointment affected his brain, and he never entirely recovered the shock. He neglected his scholars, and lost his business. He lived upon fifty pounds per annum, which his place produced, and was often in indigence. He was perfectly rational upon every subject, but the one nearest his heart ; whenever that was mentioned, he was quite insane. In the latter part of his life, he was invited by his brother to reside with him, in Ireland, where he remained till his death.

Under these preceptors Smith made so rapid a progress, that in the twentieth year of his age he composed *Teraminta*, an English opera. According to a date written in his own hand, it was finished the 11th of October, 1732, and performed in the same year. The words were written by Henry Carey.* His invention was so fertile, that in the beginning of the ensuing year, he set to music another opera called Ulysses, which was likewise peformed; the words by Humphreys.

At the age of twenty-four, Mr. Smith married the daughter of Mr. Packenham, a gentleman of good fortune, in Ireland. He had reason to suppose that she was entitled to a fortune of three thousand pounds; but he never received any portion. They lived together nearly six years, and they had several children; but none survived the age of two years. She died of a decline. Her brother was afterwards created Lord Longford.

About the age of thirty-four, he taught the grandson of old Peter Waters (whose worthless memory is recorded by Pope) : the young man appeared to form a friendship for Smith, and, succeeding to his grandfather's fortune, offered to settle on him an annuity of three hundred pounds, if he would relinquish teaching, and accompany him to the South of France, where he was going for the recovery of his health; being so great an invalid, that he was obliged to be lifted in and out of his carriage. Smith, after consulting his friends, accepted the proposal. The expectation of a good income for life, together with the

* Harry Carey composed the popular song of " God save great George our king." But although he had much genius for music, he was ignorant of the rules of composition, and applied to Smith to adapt a base to the air.

advantages which he must derive from going abroad with a sensible man, who lived in a genteel and pleasant society, induced him to throw himself on the generosity of a person, whom he conceived to be liberal, and whom he knew to be an agreeable companion. He continued with him abroad for two or three years.

It appears, from several dates annexed to his compositions, that during the three years of his residence abroad, he never intermitted his musical studies: he finished the last act of his opera of *Dario*, in 1746, and began to compose Metastasio's *Artaserse*, at Aix in Provence, in December, 1748. He passed some time at Geneva, where he formed an intimate acquaintance with some English gentlemen, distinguished for rank, learning, and talents. Among these must be particularly specified the celebrated Benjamin Stillingfleet; Mr. Price of Foxley, Herefordshire; Mr. Windham of Felbrig, in Norfolk; Mr. Aldworth Neville; Mr. Benjamin Tate of Mitcham, in Surrey; and the Rev. Dr. Dampier, afterwards Dean of Durham.

About this period Handel became blind. His surgeon, Mr. Sharp, having asked him if he was able to continue playing the organ in public, for the performance of the Oratorios? Handel replied in the negative. Sharp recommended Stanley, as a person whose memory never failed; upon which Handel burst into a loud laugh, and said, " Mr. Sharp, have you never read the Scriptures? do you not remember, if the blind lead the blind, they will both fall into the ditch?" In this dilemma, Handel sent for his pupil to assist him in the approaching Lent season. Smith could not decline Handel's invitation; and Mr. Waters resolved to return to England, as well to enjoy his friend's company, as because his sister, who was one of the party, was in a lingering and dangerous illness.

When Smith played the organ at the Theatre, during the first year of Handel's blindness, Samson was performed, and Beard sung, with great feeling,

> " Total eclipse—no sun, no moon,
> " All dark amid the blaze of noon."—

The recollection that Handel had set this air to music, with the view of the blind composer then sitting by the organ, affected the audience so forcibly, that many persons present were moved even to tears.

A year after Smith's return to England, Mrs. Waters died. A short time before her death, she advised him not to be deceived by the apparent kindness of her brother, who she knew had not named him in his will, and she much feared that he never intended to perform his promise. At her death, she left Mr. Smith five hundred pounds. In the ensuing summer, Mr. Waters proposed going to Spa, and invited Smith to accompany him, who, recollecting the intimation of Mrs. Waters, expressed apprehensions that he would not perform his promise, as he had not given him any security; upon which Waters said, angrily, " I have left you in my will the annuity I promised; won't you take my word?"—" No," replied Smith, " I would not give a pinch of snuff for your word." And, in fact, he was in the right; for Mr. Waters died within a few months, without naming Smith in his will, which had been made eight years. On this disappointment he resumed his occupation, and soon raised himself into high estimation.

At this period, Smith derived great pleasure, as well as advantage, from the friendships he had formed at Geneva. He always dwelt with extreme satisfaction on the many happy hours he had passed at Mitcham with Mr. Tate, and at Foxley with Mr. Price; from which places he dates many of his compositions. Mr. Price, whom Smith mentions as an excellent composer, encouraged him in his labours, and wrote the poetry for the Oratorio of *Judith*. At the house of Mr. Price, who had married Lord Barrington's sister, Smith became acquainted with that family; from all of whom, and particularly from Mr. Daines Barrington, he received many marks of friendship.

About this time he formed a close intimacy with Garrick, whom he often met at the house of his friend, Mr. Venables, a wine merchant, in Covent-Garden. Smith was highly delighted with the captivating manners and convivial talents of that inimitable actor; and Garrick was no less pleased with his frank and unassuming manner. Their friendship was afterwards heightened by mutual interest.

In 1754, Smith successfully displayed his talents for composition, in the Fairies, a musical drama, altered from the Midsummer-Night's Dream of Shakspeare; it was performed at the Theatre Royal Drury-lane, under the auspices of Garrick. The day before the first representation, Garrick informed Smith, that he was afraid there was a strong party to condemn the piece, because Lord Middlesex (afterwards Duke of Dorset) had taken forty places in the boxes, and so formidable a number must have some bad design. Smith replied, he could not be induced to believe Lord Middlesex had any intention to injure him, for he had never disobliged his lordship, who had always been remarkably kind to him. When the piece was performed, it proved true indeed, that Lord Middlesex had engaged so large a part of the house, but with a kind intention of supporting the piece, which had a long and continued success. The words of Shakspeare's Midsummer-Night's Dream, are light and airy, the music is well adapted to the words, and the children who performed the fairy part, were so admirably suited to the several characters, particularly Miss Young, who represented the fairy queen, that the performance was reckoned a chef-d'œuvre.

The great success of the Fairies, encouraged Smith to make another attempt in the same species of composition, by setting to music the songs in the Tempest. But although the airs were by no means inferior to those in the Fairies, yet the piece did not meet with the success it deserved; a principal cause of this failure, was probably owing to the negligent manner in which it was brought on the stage. The season was too far advanced, and the decorations were indifferent.

Smith having remonstrated against this method of proceeding, Garrick alleged that his principal actors threatened to leave him, if these musical pieces, in which they had no concern, were so frequently performed on the stage. This behaviour occasioned a breach; and their estrangement continued until Mr. Clutterbuck, a friend of both parties, persuaded Smith to forget and forgive. The two friends met at his house, and the intimacy was renewed. Thus Garrick realized that part of his character, given by Goldsmith in his excellent poem of Retaliation:—

" He cast off his friends as a huntsman his pack,

" For he knew, when he pleas'd he could whistle them back."

It must not be omitted, that when the Tempest, set to music by Purcell, was represented at the Concert of Ancient Music, the celebrated air, " Full fathom five," by Smith, was substituted for that of the original composer. It was universally admired, and has ever since been retained. This air has been harmonized as a glee by Corfe, organist of the King's chapel, with the greatest effect.

Handel continued to employ Smith senior as his treasurer, and their friendly intercourse was uninterrupted, till they both went to Tunbridge, about four years before Handel's death. But as long friendships are sometimes dissolved by the most trivial circumstances, they quarrelled there, and Smith senior left Handel in an abrupt manner, which so enraged him, that he declared he would never see him again; and though friends interfered to promote a reconciliation, their interference was for a long time without effect. After this quarrel, Handel took Smith one day by the hand, and said he was determined to put his name in the place of his father, in his will: Smith declared, if he persisted in that resolution, he would instantly quit him, and never more assist in the Oratorios; " for," added he, " what will the world think, if you set aside my father, and leave his legacy to me? they will suppose I tried, and succeeded in undermining him for my own advantage." Handel yielded to these just remonstrances.

About three weeks before Handel's death, he desired Smith junior to receive the sacrament with him. Smith asked him how he could communicate, when he was not at peace with all the world, and especially when he was at enmity with his former friend; who, though he might have offended him once, had been faithful and affectionate to him for thirty years. Handel was so much affected by this representation, that he was immediately reconciled; and dying soon after (in the year 1759), left Smith senior two thousand four hundred pounds, having before given him one thousand pounds. To Mr. Smith he left all his manuscript music* in score, his harpsichord, on which almost all that music had been composed, his portrait painted by Denner, and his bust by Roubillac.

It had been Handel's wish, that all the manuscript music should be assigned to Oxford, and preserved in the university library; and with that attention to his posthumous fame, and regard to an university which had been sensible of his merits, he proposed to give Smith a legacy of three thousand pounds, if he would resign his claim to the promise which Handel had made to him. But he had too much enthusiasm for the art, and too great a veneration for the production of so able a composer, his friend and instructor, to relinquish, for any pecuniary consideration, so inestimable a prize; and Handel faithfully fulfilled his promise at his death. Many of Handel's compositions were afterwards pirated from scores lent by Smith, and from others which had not been returned by performers. Too inattentive to his own advantage, he never prosecuted the printers, and many editions were published.

---

* The Great Frederick, King of Prussia, offered Smith two thousand pounds for Handel's manuscripts; but he was unwilling to let such a treasure go out of England.

Smith, after Handel's death, carried on the Oratorios in partnership with Mr. Stanley,* whose professional abilities, and estimable

* John Stanley was born in 1713. His father had a lucrative employment in the Post-office. In his second year he became blind by the following circumstance:—he fell down with a china bason in his hand; the bason breaking, a pointed fragment cut through one of his eyes, which occasioned the loss of the other.

Having attained the age of seven, he began to learn music; not because he had discovered the smallest propensity to it, or because his father was musical himself, or fond of the art: he was advised to have his son instructed on the harpsichord as an amusement, to which he consented; but without any hopes that it would be advantageous to his progress in life. His first master was Reading, a scholar of Blow, and organist of Hackney. He continued under Reading only a few months; during which time, the difficulty of receiving information was so great, that he made scarcely any progress. The boy, however, discovering great pleasure in the occupation, his father placed him with Dr. Green, organist of St. Paul's.

Under this scientific master Stanley made a most rapid progress, and attained so great a proficiency, that when eleven, he was chosen organist of the church of Allhallows, Bread-street; at fourteen, he was appointed organist of St. Andrew's, Holborn, in preference to a great number of candidates; at sixteen, he was elected by the Honourable Society of the Middle Temple, one of their organists. These two places he retained to his death. His abilities as a master acquired him a handsome income. He had great facility in teaching; and from his patience in instructing, and his address, was always much beloved by his pupils.

" Few persons," observes Dr. Burney, " have passed a more active life in every branch of his art, than this extraordinary musician; having been not only a neat, pleasing, and accurate performer, but a natural and agreeable composer, and an intelligent instructor. He continued to teach until 1760; when, on the death of Handel, he entered into an engagement with Smith, to carry on the Oratorios for fourteen years. At the end of that time, Smith retiring from the musical world, Stanley engaged with Mr.

character, rendered him a very desirable associate.   On the decease of his father, Smith declined receiving any share of the small fortune, which was left among his three children, and divided it between his two sisters.

It was Mr. Smith's peculiar turn of disposition, not to live much with the professors of music, Pepusch, Roseingrave, and Handel excepted ; and the friendships he formed in life were with men of a different profession, or persons of fortune, character, and abilities.

Linley for the same purpose, and was honoured with the patronage of their Majesties. In 1785, his health being much impaired, he retired from business. He died the 19th of May, 1786."

He was a most cheerful and lively companion, of a placid and serene temper, and perfectly contented with his situation.   He was often heard to say, that he would not receive his sight, if it was in his power.   He felt himself, he said, perfectly happy under his present circumstances ; and should have so much to learn and unlearn, that all would be uncertainty and confusion.

The loss of his sight was amply repaid by the acuteness of his hearing, and the extreme sensibility of his touch.   He could find his way even through the narrowest passages and alleys of London ; he could ascertain the size of an apartment by the sound of his voice ; he recollected the voices of those whom he had not seen for many years ; and he played at whist with a facility that astonished all who saw him.   The cards were marked with a needle at one corner ; but the marks were so small as to be almost imperceptible ; yet he was never embarrassed, and required only that the card which was played should be mentioned.   He was fond of riding, and an excellent judge of horses : he discovered the proportions by feeling, and judged of its paces by the ear ; and he once prevented a friend from purchasing a horse that was lame.   He married Miss Harland, daughter of Captain Harland, in the East India service, by whom he had no issue.

Among those with whom he was closely connected, was Dr. Coxe,* Physician Extraordinary to the King; who was highly noticed for his professional abilities, and much beloved and esteemed for his amiable virtues and private character. The friendship which the Doctor entertained for Mr. Smith, and the high opinion which he formed of his integrity, was so great, that on his death bed, he recommended his wife to consult Mr. Smith on every emergency.

Desirous of proving his good wishes for the welfare of her family, anxious to render every assistance in his power, and convinced that his principles of good will could not be carried into effect, without a closer alliance than that of friendship, at a proper season he proposed himself to her in marriage, that he might be at once, and effectually, a father to her children. Her consent was succeeded by the most unequivocal demonstrations of the generosity and candour of his declarations. His kindness to all her children, invariably, in sickness and in health, his anxiety for their welfare, his wish to further their interest, his readiness to promote it, his satisfaction at every little advantage that accrued to them, were convincing indications of a kind and affectionate heart.

Soon after the accession of his present Majesty, Mr. Smith was introduced to the Royal Family. His introduction was principally occasioned by the following circumstance: Pinchbeck being employed by the Earl of Bute to construct a barrel organ of extraordinary

---

* Dr. Coxe was distinguished by Mr. Melmoth's elegant pen, in his Fitzosborne's Letters, under the name of Philotes; and his wife, who afterwards espoused Mr. Smith, was mentioned under the appellation of Aspasia.

size, requested Smith to superintend the work; which he at first declined, but, on application from his Lordship, afterwards complied. Langshaw, a very ingenious artist, was employed; and, under Smith's directions, set the barrels with so much delicacy and taste, as to convey a warm idea of the impression which the hand gives on the instrument. The organ* was esteemed a masterpiece in musical mechanism; and Lord Bute was so well pleased with his success, that he was desirous of making an adequate compensation for the trouble. Smith declined all pecuniary gratification; and hinted, that he should think his pains more than amply repaid, if, through his Lordship's recommendation, the King would condescend to patronize the Oratorios. Lord Bute accordingly represented Mr. Smith in so favourable a light, that the King honoured the Oratorios with his presence; at first, six nights out of eleven; afterwards, for several years, he went the whole eleven, which was a great support, and brought much company to the house, although the Oratorios had then ceased to be the favourite entertainment of the public; his Majesty almost *stood single* in his approbation of the great Handel, when the preference for Italian music was becoming universal.

The Princess Dowager of Wales having expressed an inclination to engage some person of eminence in the musical profession, to attend twice a week, and give her instruction on the harpsichord, Lord Bute said, that he would recommend a master, who he was sure would be acceptable; but before he could name him, her Royal Highness inter-

* The size of the barrels was considerably larger than any that had been made. The organ itself was also much larger than had ever been used for barrels. After the death of the Earl of Bute, this organ was purchased by the Earl of Shaftesbury.

rupting him, said, she had already fixed on a person; and immediately mentioned Mr. Smith. He was accordingly placed in the Princess's household, and attended at Carlton House once or twice a week, with a salary of two hundred pounds.

The Princess was uncommonly gracious and condescending, and derived so much satisfaction and improvement from his instructions, that she was often heard to say, that in her advanced age, she had acquired a new taste for music, and had received notions of harmony, which she had never before experienced. She was fond of his musical compositions, and several of them, particularly the Oratorio of Gideon, were performed at Carlton House.

In 1772 he lost his great benefactress, and was deeply affected. To relieve his mind he undertook a task, suitable to the melancholy occasion. He set the funeral service to music, which he had long meditated; and his mind was so occupied, that during several nights he enjoyed no rest. It is composed with great pathos and expression.

After the death of the Princess Dowager, the King graciously continued to Mr. Smith the same pension out of his privy purse, free of all deductions, which greatly contributed to the ease and comfort of his life.

In a mind so constituted as that of Mr. Smith, where liberality and disinterestedness were distinguishing features, it is easy to be supposed that gratitude would be no less conspicuous; and that the conduct of the King, in graciously patronizing the Oratorios, his condescension to him, whenever he was honoured with an audience, and his conti nuing to him the pension of two hundred pounds, paid by the Princess Dowager of Wales, and drawn from the privy purse (free from all customary deductions), and that pension graciously presented to him from his Majesty's own hand, would naturally operate on a disposition peculiarly sensible. He accordingly expressed that gratitude in a way which he thought most acceptable to his Sovereign; and in the fulness of his heartfelt acknowledgment, presented to the King the rich legacy which Handel had left him, of all his manuscript music, in score. The harpsichord, so remarkable for the ivory being indented by Handel's continued exertions, and on which, as has been already related, the far greater part of his music had been composed; and his bust, by Roubillac, he sent afterwards to Windsor Castle. Of all that his great instructor had bequeathed him, he only reserved to himself the portrait painted by Denner.

The produce from the Oratorios answered Mr. Smith's expectations every year, and in 1769, when Miss Linley sung, the advantage was increased in a great degree. But when she declined singing in public, and the King was prevented from appearing in public, by the Queen's lying-in during Lent, the Oratorios were much deserted, and performed almost to empty houses. Smith therefore, thought it most advisable to resign the conduct of these performances, lest, by persisting, he should have the misfortune to lose what he had formerly gained. He quitted the neighbourhood of London, and retired to a house he had recently bought, in Brock-street, Bath.

In 1785, Mrs. Smith died. Mr. Smith, who had ever been tenderly attached to her, was most severely afflicted at her loss. Grief so shook his frame that he appeared visibly declining, but the strength of his constitution enabled him to recover this blow. He lived beloved and respected from his benevolence, which led him on all occasions to assist the distressed, as far as his moderate fortune permitted; and he frequently denied himself gratifications and indulgences, that by these little sacrifices he might be able to relieve the necessitous. His benevolence made him take pleasure in improving young people; and at the advanced age of eighty-one, he instructed a few young ladies who had genius for music.

Several persons of high rank and merit, who had formerly known him, usually called upon him when they came to Bath, and expressed their regard for him, as a man equally respectable for genius and integrity. He used to observe upon these occasions,—" I am in general dead to the vanities of the world, but I own myself flattered by these marks of attention: there was a time when I was courted, because I could amuse and entertain; but now the attention that is shewn me, when I can give no entertainment, can only arise from the esteem that the world pays to my character."

In September, 1795, Smith was seized with a disorder, which terminated his existence in eight days. At first he suffered great pain, but being relieved by opiates, remained in a state of composure. From the first moment of his illness, to the instant of his death, he displayed the brightest example of a true Christian and a benevolent mind. He expired on the third of October, in the eighty-fifth year of his age.

Smith's last effort of composition was the Redemption, an Oratorio compiled from the Scriptures, by the Reverend William Coxe. It was intended for public performance, but the difficulty of procuring proper voices frustrated the plan.

Although a great enthusiast in his profession, yet after his retirement, he seldom amused himself at the harpsichord. He did not, however, desist from his usual application either from satiety, disgust, or want of feeling, but rather from extreme sensibility. His style of playing was singularly animated and impressive, and his mind was totally absorbed in his occupation. But when age had produced such a tremor of the hands, as prevented him from executing light and delicate passages, he felt so much mortification on finding his inability to touch the instrument in his accustomed manner, and to produce an effect corresponding with his exquisite feelings, that he thought it prudent to relinquish his favourite employment.

When the Commemoration of Handel was celebrated with such wonderful effect in Westminster Abbey, under the direction of Joah Bates, Esq. the King was desirous that Smith should be present at the performance, and sent him a gracious and pressing invitation to come to London for that purpose. His Majesty assured him that he should be admitted without difficulty into a commodious seat in the Abbey, and that he should receive every accommodation during his residence in town. Smith was fully sensible of this gracious mark of condescension; but declined the honour with reluctance, apprehensive that from his advanced age, so exquisitely powerful a performance of the works of his great master, would excite such emotions as might too much affect his feeble frame.

As a professional man, he was unobtrusive. His talents were no less solid than brilliant; equally adapted to the fanciful and elegant style of composition, exemplified in the opera of the Fairies, and to the serious cast of sacred music, displayed in his Oratorios and Funeral Anthem.

With a quiet but not inactive turn of mind, he did not pursue the exertion of his faculties unremittingly to his own profit. From constitution he was of a tranquil disposition, little calculated to struggle against the intrigues which modest merit must encounter in a science in which the professors, as well as performers, too often appear peculiarly irritable, and,

——— " too fond to rule alone,
" Bear, like the Turk, no brother near the throne."

Though he loved the art, he found himself unequal to the trade, and had not courage to encounter obstacles, or patience to reconcile contending interests.

His spirit was so liberal and independent, that he could never bend to the circumstances of the times, nor sufficiently consult the taste of the age, if he deemed that taste frivolous or capricious : he could not be induced to sacrifice his own feelings and judgment to expected profit.

His Operas of the Fairies and the Tempest, Lessons for the Harpsichord, and the Oratorio of Paradise Lost, are the chief productions with which the world is acquainted. A list of his works is given in the Appendix

But if his own compositions did not sufficiently speak for him, his highest commendation would be the praise of Handel. To have been called upon by that great musician to supply his place at the organ, testifies his abilities as a performer, and conductor of a band.

His genius was by no means confined to music; he was fond of reading, had a taste for all the liberal arts, and formed a small but interesting collection of pictures.

In stature, Mr. Smith was below the middle size; he was upright in his walk, polite in his address; had hands delicately formed, blue and impressive eyes, and his whole countenance remarkably open. Though naturally grave, he was alive to cheerful conversation. His laugh was peculiarly unrestrained; not loud and boisterous, but indicating that heartfelt satisfaction which surrenders the understanding, without folly, to the cheerful and social impulse of the moment.

In his private character, he united many estimable and agreeable qualities; he was sincere, benevolent, and humane; scrupulously just in all moral obligations, and had a devout sense of religion, untinctured by superstition. In society he was cheerful, and his conversation was enlivened with pleasant sallies and quick repartee. In domestic life he was benevolent and affectionate; and was kind, almost to a fault, to his domestics. The same principle remained with him in the hour of sickness and of death; as he was anxious in his last moments to spare his attendants all unnecessary trouble.

He was particularly careful to impress on the minds of his adopted children, a full conviction that Christianity is alone sufficient to happiness; and that a disbelief of divine revelation would insensibly lead to every species of vice and misery. A letter which he wrote twenty years before his death to one of his adopted sons, when at the university, fully proves that this principle was not dictated by sickness or old age, but was the genuine result of firm conviction and settled belief.

" My dear Friend,

" I am much obliged to you for your affectionate letter, as it con firmed me in the opinion I always had, of the goodness and rectitude of your heart, which I hope you will always preserve; and which, give me leave to say, is no very easy task in so degenerate an age as that we live in at present. Much of your future happiness will, in a great measure, depend on the choice you make of friends; you must be particularly careful in so nice a point; for it is not sufficient his being barely a good moral man, that will qualify him for your friendship, there is still something more required, and that is, he ought to be a Christian; and unless he has really those principles in him, you cannot safely take him to your bosom: for although he would not wrong you of a farthing, yet he will not scruple (if he be an Atheist or Deist) to endeavour with great pains to imbibe into you principles, that will not only make you very unhappy in this life, but, what is worse, hazard your eternal salvation in the next.

" My dear friend, I have only cautioned you against one set of men, and to me the most dangerous; others may lead you into many indiscretions, but not so fatal in their consequences. All that I have farther to say at present is, that I hope on all occasions you will look on me as your sincere friend, and not hide any part of your conduct from me; and in return for such a confidence reposed, I will promise you, that it will be the pleasure and study of my life to make yours as happy as I possibly can.

I am, my dear friend,

Most affectionately yours,

J. C. SMITH."

In the last years of his life he was particularly careful to soften his manners, to correct his temper, and to render himself as faultless as possible. He verified that maxim of his favourite Madame de Sevigné, " Quand on n'est plus jeune, c'est alors qu'il faut se perfectionner, et tâcher de regagner, par les bonnes qualités, ce qu'on perd du côté des agréables,"

His life was extended beyond the common period of human existence, without deviating from the paths of integrity and honour. The testimony of several who were his contemporaries in the early season of his days, and of many who were witnesses, at a later period,

" To the noiseless tenour of his way,"

who saw and conversed with him daily, who are still living, and can appreciate his merits, may be adduced as a proof of this assertion.

APPENDIX.

LIST

OF

MR. SMITH'S COMPOSITIONS,

IN THE POSSESSION OF HIS DAUGHTER-IN-LAW, LADY RIVERS.

ENGLISH OPERAS.

Teraminta, an Opera. Three Acts. *Composed by J. C. Smith, Oct.* 11, 1732. Performed the same year. The words by Henry Carey.

Ulysses, an Opera. *Composed by J. C. Smith, April* 11, 1733. Performed the same year. The words by Mr. Humphreys.

The Fairies; or Midsummer-Night's Dream, an Opera. Three Acts. Published, 1756. The words principally taken from Shakspeare, said to be by Garrick.

The Tempest. Three Acts. Published, 1756. From Shakspeare. The words said to be by Garrick.

Medea; only two Acts finished. The words by Mr. Stillingfleet.

ITALIAN OPERAS.

Dario. *Fine de l'Atto primo, London, March* 8, 1746. *Fine de l'Atto secondo, London, June* 6, 1746. *Fine de l'Atto terzo, Rotterdam, Sept.* 5, 1746.

Issipile. 1746.

Il Ciro Riconosciuto. Three Acts. Words by Metastasio. No date or signature.

ORATORIOS.

Paradise Lost. Three Parts. Words by Stillingfleet. *Mitcham, December* 1, 1757. *Finished at Foxley, July* 29, 1758. Dr. Burney says it was performed in 1760.

David's Lamentation over Saul and Jonathan. *Composed by J. C. Smith, March* 20, 1738. Burney says it was performed in 1748.

ORATORIOS.

Nabal. Words by Dr. Morell. Performed in 1764. Compiled partly from
Handel.

Gideon. 1769. Words by Dr. Morell.
Compiled partly from Handel.

Judith, in Three Acts. Words by the
late Mr. Price. Thus noted by Mr. Smith:
*By Robert Price, Esq. of Foxley, in He-
refordshire: who was himself an excellent
composer in music.*

Jehosaphat. Two Acts. I can find
no trace that this Oratorio was ever performed.

Redemption. Three Acts. Never performed. Words from the Scripture, by
the Rev. W. Coxe.

MISCELLANEOUS.

The Burial Service.

Winter: or Daphne. Pope's Pastoral
on the death of Mrs. Tempest. *Jan.* 26,
1746.

The Seasons. Two Parts.

Fugues, 1754, 1756. Never published.

Lessons for the Harpsichord, published.

Thamesi, Isi, e Proteo. In honour of
Frederick Prince of Wales.

FRAGMENTS.

A few scenes of Artaserse, by Metastasio. Dated in Mr. Smith's hand writing, *Aix en Provence,* 1749.

A Hunting Scene and Song, composed
for Queen Caroline's Hermitage; but
without date or note.

DUETT from the ORATORIO
of
David's Lamentation over Saul and Jonathan.

Larghetto

Sad

2

pride, On yon high Moun _ _ _ _ _ _ _ _ _ _ tain bleed _ _ _

pride,   On yon high Moun _ _ _ tain bleed _ _

_ _ _ _ _ _ ing lies   On yon high Mountain bleeding lies _ _ _

_ _ _ _ _ ing lies   On yon high Mountain bleeding lies _ _ _

moun - - - - tain - bleeding lies - - -

- - - - - - - - - - tain bleeding lies - - -

on yon high mountain bleeding lies

- - - - - on yon high mountain bleeding lies

died no weeping friend to close their eyes

no weeping friend to close their eyes How

How have the mighty warriors died How

have the mighty warriors died How have the mighty warriors

Song from the Opera of
MEDEA

Bid her learn the gentler Arts Such as footh and

conquer hearts Softnefs is fair wo _ mans

Dower   that a _ _ lone can give her power   that _ _ _ a _

_ lone _ _ can give her power

She who lays that charm a-side falls a

Victim to her pride

15

Recitative and Air from the Oratorio of
JUDITH

Oh rash presumtuous man; how hast thou

dar'd to bind the Counsels of the Lord; unskill'd to

fathom the weak shallow heart of man; how canst thou search out

God; and Comprehend his vast de‐signs; for not within the bounds of

these five days alone, but ev'ry day he may defend us.

or he may destroy. mean time my friends

let us lift up our hearts in thanks to him who thus has deignd to

try us. as of old he tried our fathers

Andantino

With Resignation let us wait the hour when

sorrow shall be turnd to mirth nor vainly think to circumscribe that

Pow'r to which Crea _ tion owes its birth to which Cre _ _ _ ation

owes its birth

With Re_fig__nation let us wait   with Re_fig__nation let us

wait when forrow fhall be turnd be turnd to mirth be turnd to mirth

Nor vainly think nor vainly think to circum_scribe that powr to which Cre_

_ _ ation owes its birth with Resignation let us wait the hour nor vainly think to

cir _ _ cumscribe that pow'r to which Cre _ ation owes its birth to

which Cre _ a _ tion owes its birth.

LARGO

Shall human Reason dare to scan and limit Pow'r di_

_vine And shall that help__lefs Crea__ture Man Om_

_ni_potence con__fine Om__ni_potence con_fine With_

Da Capo al Segno

AIR

ANDANTE

Dando

Impero al gus-to al Prode L'Ilom sol gode la Li _ber ta L'Ilom sol gode la

liber_ta Lll sol go _ _ _ de liber__ta

la liber_ta la liber_ta _ _ _ _

ta li _ ber _ ta   Dando

impero al giusto al Prode   L'llom ſol gode li _ ber _ ta _ _ _

L'llom ſol gode ſolo ſolo gode ſol liber _

Alle Leggi sta som messo ch egli

stessoallor si fa — — — — ch egli stesso allor

si fachegli stessoallor si fa

Dando im

Da Capo al Segno ℔

My hope is in thee O Lord thou art swift to comfort

and wilt have mercy up——on thy afflicted Preserve me O

Lord for in thee have I put my Trust.

Hautboi SOLO

Violini Andantino

Andantino

Thou art my

wa........tersof Com.....fort

Thou art my Shepherd thou wilt feed me thouwilt feed me   in a green

Pasture   thouwilt feed me in a green Pas.............